Praise for Levy's *Pretreatment Guide for Homeless Outreach & Housing First*

"Recently, Barbara Poppe, Executive Director for the U.S. Interagency Council on Homelessness (ICH) issued a challenge to Continuum of Care & Ten-Year Plan Leaders:

> 'Today I want to address chronic homelessness, which is the first goal in Opening Doors. We have fewer than 1,000 days to bring the number of people experiencing chronic homelessness to zero; every day and every minute counts. For people living with disabilities and disabling conditions, every day or minute spent on the streets is another day or minute spent struggling to survive.'

As one of these leaders and someone with 25 years of providing services to the homeless population, I felt that I had the answer to Ms. Poppe's call to action; Mr. Levy's book! As with his earlier works, Jay Levy engages the reader with poignant narratives of this extremely vulnerable group of people then, in this latest work, chapter by chapter builds an effective framework for truly solving this decade's old social dilemma. I strongly recommend this book to anyone truly vested in Ending Chronic Homelessness."

Jerry Ray, Director of Homeless Services
Mental Health Association Inc. (Springfield, MA)

"Jay Levy has now advanced his work with the chronically homeless into a comprehensive book. His *Pretreatment Guide for Homeless Outreach & Housing First* codifies his previous efforts and expands the knowledge base by providing new insights into helping and housing chronically homeless couples, unaccompanied youth and adults.

Through Jay Levy's work, a cadre of social service workers and housing providers have come to better understand and adopt the principles of a housing first strategy and the importance of pretreatment model in the continuing struggle to end homelessness."

David W. Modzelewski, Housing Coordinator
Western Massachusetts Regional Network to End Homelessness

"*Pretreatment Guide for Homeless Outreach & Housing First* is essential reading to both people new to the movement to end homelessness and folks who have been in the trenches for many years. Learn how to do effective outreach with the chronic homeless population, and the ins and outs of the Housing First model. The personal stories and the success cases will give inspiration to work even harder to help both individuals and for ending homelessness in your community."

Michael Stoops, Director of Community Organizing
National Coalition for the Homeless, Washington, DC

"*Pretreatment Guide for Homeless Outreach & Housing First* could be a text book for a course on working with chronically homeless people. It is a hands-on manual full of caring, compassion and decency. The principles here applied to homeless people are those that should guide all helping relationships such as psychotherapy and social work. This is actually best expressed in the opening sentence of the last chapter: 'A pretreatment guide based on universal principles of care has been presented and applied to Homeless Outreach and Housing First activities.' It is all evidence-based, and the author's expertise shines through.

A really valuable aspect of this book is the level of detail in the case studies. This makes it a primer for inexperienced therapists and social workers. Equally useful is the way in which the same principles are applied in different circumstances, cumulatively adding to their understanding. This is always fresh, never boring."

Bob Rich, PhD, AnxietyAndDepression-Help.com

Pretreatment Guide for Homeless Outreach & Housing First

Helping Couples, Youth, and Unaccompanied Adults

Jay S. Levy, MSW, LICSW

Foreword by David W. Havens, M.Ed.

Loving Healing Press

Library of Congress Cataloging-in-Publication Data

Levy, Jay S., 1961-
 Pretreatment guide for homeless outreach & housing first :
helping couples, youth, and unaccompanied adults / Jay S. Levy,
MSW, LICSW ; foreword by David Havens.
  pages cm
 Includes bibliographical references and index.
  ISBN 978-1-61599-201-0 (trade paper : alk. paper) -- ISBN 978-
1-61599-202-7 (hardcover : alk. paper) -- ISBN 978-1-61599-
203-4 (ebook)
  1. Homeless persons--Housing--United States. 2. Homeless
persons--Services for--United States. I. Title.
  HD7287.96.U6L48 2013
  363.5--dc23
                                                2013021591

Published by
Loving Healing Press Inc.
5145 Pontiac Trail
Ann Arbor, MI 48105

info@LHPress.com
Tollfree 888-761-6268
FAX 734-663-6861

Distributed by Ingram Book Group (USA/CAN), Bertram's
Books (UK).

Dedication

I dedicate this project to people without homes, and to all those who have survived homelessness, and to the outreach workers who help the most vulnerable among us. May their courage, strength and dedication serve as an inspiration to others.

Proceeds from this Book

The Author has pledged 25% of book royalties, and other related book profits, to a 501c(3) charity (e.g. National Coalition for the Homeless) that supports the cause of ending chronic homelessness.

2/6/16

Rosie,

Thanks to you + your daughter
for supporting the cause!

All the best,

Jay

Contents

Tables and Figures

Acknowledgments

I am indebted to my wife Louise for her love, patience, wisdom, and willingness to listen and critically respond. Thanks to my daughters, Talia and Sara, for taking the time to talk and play, while reminding me of teenage angst, rebellion, and their excitement for life. Thanks to Dave Havens for overseeing the REACH Housing First project and taking the time, care, and effort to compose the foreword. Additional thanks goes to Larry Gottlieb, Dave Modzelewski, and Jerry Ray for their tireless efforts to develop new and innovative programs to better serve chronically homeless individuals. Thanks to Eliot CHS-PATH Outreach and C-SPECH Housing First staff who on a day-to-day basis continue to help those who are most in need. Finally, and most importantly, thanks to my mom for making all things possible.

Permissions

Portions of this book have previously appeared in *Homeless Outreach & Housing First: Lessons Learned* (monograph), as well as in *Homeless Narratives & Pretreatment Pathways: From Words to Housing*. Specifically, "Ronald's Narrative" (Ch. 2) and "Reasons for Ending Chronic Homelessness" (Ch. 3) were reworked from the monograph, while "Lacey's Narrative" (Ch. 6) and portions of "Housing First" (Ch. 9) and "Supervision" (Ch. 11) were reprinted from my book *Homeless Narratives & Pretreatment Pathways*. The addendum interview was previously published in the *Journal of Humanitarian Affairs* (GHNN). Thanks to Victor R. Volkman and Ernest Dempsey for encouraging my writing and granting permission to reprint these sections.

Confidentiality

The homeless narratives depicted in this work are based on actual persons and events from my experiences as an outreach counselor. However, names, places, and events have been altered to protect client confidentiality.

Foreword – The REACH Housing First Pilot

The State medical examiner had just revealed his findings that a homeless man had been discovered deceased in an abandoned building in Springfield, and that his body showed signs of extensive flea infestation. The City Council committee that received the information ignored the glaring lack of service connections for this person, and instead responded to this tragic occurrence by publicly setting the full enforcement capacity of the City's Code & Inspections Department upon any residential program serving persons with developmental disabilities, mental illnesses, addictions, domestic violence and homelessness. Suddenly, our efforts to determine how to provide substantial real help to people experiencing long-term homelessness and living on the streets shifted from a moral and intellectual challenge to a practical and political necessity. Thankfully, a political resolution was found and ended this misdirected hyper-enforcement against the residential components of the City's human service sector. Afterward, homeless advocates struggled to find a way to promote safety by better caring for the underserved and hardest to reach people within our region. As it was the mid-1980s, there was a significant gap in our knowledge and practice, as well as the need to discover new effective ways for connecting with homeless persons who did not fit or could not access the traditional outpatient, residential, or shelter models of service.

Fortunately, in 2013, Jay S. Levy provides us with his *Pretreatment Guide for Homeless Outreach & Housing First* to share his pretreatment practices and principles, scholarly review, history, wisdom, values, and practical lessons learned. Further, through extensive presentation and exploration of *Homeless Outreach and Housing First* case narratives, the reader is given a "hands on" approach for serving the chronically homeless. Jay has also advanced the local capacity to serve the long-term homeless by participating in community efforts to create innovative approaches for providing "Housing First Programs" in Western Massachusetts.

One of the programs Jay Levy helped to make a reality is the Regional Engagement and Assessment of the Chronically Homeless (REACH) Pilot Program.

The REACH Pilot was established to determine if it was possible to use a Housing First approach connected to an outreach component to serve chronically homeless persons who by history present as the least ready for housing. It primarily targeted an unsheltered homeless population, and 94% of its participants simultaneously struggled with mental illness, addiction, and a major medical condition. The REACH experience determined that Housing First does work for this so called difficult-to-house population, provided there are intensive on-going relationship-centered supports using the pretreatment principles described in this publication, which includes assertively supporting transitions. REACH Housing retention over a 5 year period of time was greater than 85%. This compares favorably with other residential programs that serve chronically homeless individuals. Of the 18 participants who were housed, only two persons failed to sustain themselves in permanent housing over the program's first 5 years. One other participant finally achieved housing stability outside of the REACH Program, after the program continued to assist with access to services that contributed to eventual housing stability.

A program outcome that was not anticipated was that the most common reason for a participant exiting REACH housing was a health related issue that involved transition to age/health related higher levels of residential care within the traditional health system. The second most common cause of exit was natural death related to existing chronic health conditions. Remarkably, participants entering the REACH Pilot averaged over 8 years of homelessness, and yet the vast majority successfully maintained their permanent housing.

The Mental Health Association Inc. staff who worked on the REACH project are grateful for the many community supports that made it possible to provide such an innovative Housing First opportunity. The program greatly benefited from our association with Jay S. Levy and his knowledge and ongoing consultation via monthly REACH meetings. I encourage anyone working with homeless persons to make good use of the well-developed, practical approach that Jay provides in this work.

> David W. Havens, M.Ed., Program Director: Homeless
> Housing/Safe Havens, Mental Health Association, Inc.

Preface – Unveiling the Message: From Monograph to Book

My writing and field work began with a basic question. How can we help people experiencing long-term homelessness to get housed? I've come to realize that accessing income and affordable housing are central, while fostering connections with others and developing a life with meaningful structure play an integral role in resolving the debilitating effects of chronic homelessness. The overall goal is to have a home, which encompasses not only being housed and part of a community, but also includes the stability of a long-term tenancy and the prospect of improved health. There is no shortcut to achieving this. It is relationship-based work that meets people "where they are at" and takes on the challenges and obstacles they have endured. Finding pathways to housing, improved health and meaningful structure needs to take place on both systemic and individual levels.

The outreach worker is the guide, and the travel is rarely if ever a straight path. Its success hinges on two people developing a trusting relationship and an effective communication that becomes goal centered, while always believing in the possible. This is at the heart of pretreatment. Both Homeless Outreach and Housing First are relationship-based endeavors that demand a sense of optimism, but also benefit from a proven client-centered method (Rogers, 1957; Wampold 2001) of helping others. When viewing things through the lens of a pretreatment perspective, it is evident that there is an important interconnection between *Homeless Outreach* and *Housing First* activities.

There are three keys to pretreatment:

1. Our initial task is to get where the client is at

2. Interventions are informed by how our words and actions resonate in the client's world

3. A trusting relationship between worker and client is the foundation of our work, while common language construction is the main tool for facilitating positive change.

The experience of doing Homeless Outreach throughout the 1980s and 90s brought me in direct contact with the multiple systemic barriers and the personal indignities that individuals without homes faced. The sad reality is that people experiencing long-term homelessness, poverty and major disabilities are often expected to denounce who they are and what they value, before they are deemed "ready for help." It was not uncommon for people with major mental illnesses and/or addictions to be denied access to housing with support services unless they were ready to enroll and comply with treatment. Unfortunately many folks with major mental illnesses or co-occurring disorders were in denial of the severity of their issues, or defined themselves in ways that did not include the concepts of mental illness or addiction. They therefore felt that treatment was unnecessary or even harmful. This resulted in some people either being denied entrance to residential programs or refusing to give it a try. They therefore remained at serious risk due to continued homelessness and lack of treatment for serious mental health, addiction, and medical issues.

In response to this dilemma, I began to research and read the latest information on homelessness via human service journals, as well as shared and compared what worked in the field with other outreach workers. Most importantly, people without homes often gave me direct feedback as to what services, resources, and interventions were most effective. Through my writing I was able to integrate these new insights with clinical approaches from my field experience and with ideas from my educational background of philosophy, psychology, and social work. This evolving wisdom began to bear fruit after several years. Even though my writing was initially fueled by anger and frustration, I quickly came to realize the power of the pen.

I first introduced a pretreatment model and its five guiding principles by publishing several case studies via Social Work journals (1998-2004). This became the basis for my first book (2010) *Homeless Narratives & Pretreatment Pathways: From Words to Housing*. It shares people's stories of survival, meaning-making, and overcoming homelessness, while providing a pretreatment approach for helping those who are most in need. *Homeless*

Narratives & Pretreatment Pathways has been recommended by the National Coalition for the Homeless, and the Massachusetts Housing and Shelter Alliance among others. During the autumn of 2011, I released a monograph (educational booklet) entitled *Homeless Outreach & Housing First: Lessons Learned*. The monograph features three written works that explore the relationship between Homeless Outreach and Housing First. The monograph found its niche as a quick and easy guide for both Homeless Outreach and Housing First staff, as well as with other interested parties (e.g., concerned citizens). Even though it was limited in size, people appreciated its direct applications, case illustrations and straightforward approach to helping.

This led to the current project of expanding the monograph into a book. I greatly expanded its volume and scope, and reworked previously published chapters. This document now includes, among other things, the exploration of how meaning-making interfaces with homelessness and the essential client-worker task of common language construction, reflections on youth homelessness, how to best work with untreated dually diagnosed individuals (SA/MI), as well as providing new stories such as Janice & Michael's Narrative – Helping Homeless Couples. As with the monograph, the focus remains on a shared vision of Homeless Outreach and Housing First activities.

This book provides a rich and fertile educational resource for learning and reflection on how to address the vexing problem of chronic homelessness. I hope the reader finds value in both the pretreatment guide and "hands on" interventions that are offered by sharing people's stories of homelessness and beyond. Effective outreach principles, strategies and interventions based on a pretreatment model of care can be applied before and after someone is housed. If we really want to significantly reduce long term homelessness, then we need to bring together quality outreach services and affordable housing options so the most vulnerable among us can achieve a sense of community, dignity and meaning, while safely living in their homes.

Chapter 1 – Pretreatment Considerations for Homeless Outreach & Housing First

> "The most important human endeavor is the striving for morality in our actions. Our inner balance and even our very existence depend on it."
> – Albert Einstein (1950)

Over the past 20 years, efforts have become more focused toward significantly reducing, or perhaps even ending chronic homelessness among unaccompanied adults. This began on a national level with the development of outreach teams across the US, which are currently supported by both federal and state dollars – most notably via PATH outreach teams (Projects for Assistance in Transitions from Homelessness) and Healthcare for the Homeless projects. Tireless advocacy by groups like the National Coalition for the Homeless and the National Alliance to End Homelessness have been crucial toward galvanizing support for proven practices and policies necessary to end or significantly reduce homelessness. These efforts have continued, and in many respects have matured via the US Interagency Council on Homelessness and the Department of Housing and Urban Development (HUD). Targeted federal and state funds have been used to develop affordable housing resources, Housing First initiatives, and the formation of community based regional and/or Continuum of Care networks. Communities and larger geographical regions now have specific plans that address resource, access and prevention issues, as well as supporting and utilizing research to inform best practices. In many places, outreach teams and shelter staff have direct and improved access to housing resources. Some strides have been made toward providing housing plus support services for those most in need. Nevertheless, serious challenges remain and every day the health and safety of many people experiencing homelessness are at considerable risk.

Throughout my career, I have worked very closely with outreach teams, shelter staff, residential programs, and Housing First initiatives. There is a fundamental relationship between *Homeless Outreach* and *Housing First*. Homeless Outreach is an essential step toward meeting people experiencing long-term or episodic (multiple episodes) homelessness. It is the means for developing the critical trusting relationships necessary for supporting transitions to affordable housing and/or needed treatment. The greater our success in implementing Housing First, the more our need for high quality outreach-based support services that promote housing stabilization. We have seen a major shift over time. Some of the formerly hardest to reach folks are now successfully housed, but still have chronic medical, mental health, and substance abuse issues that negatively impact their overall sense of health and wellbeing, including their ability to effectively connect with their neighbors and community.

Whether we are providing Homeless Outreach or housing stabilization services for people with longstanding difficulties, the central challenges remain the same. It all begins with the formation of a trusting relationship. Whether outreach is done on the streets or in an apartment, the helping process is always interpersonal. Our hope is that two people, who are often from vastly different worlds and experiences, can come together to successfully work on mutually agreed goals to bring about positive change. It is important that we recognize that it is the client who has ownership of the objectives that are at the center of our work. Ultimately, much depends on building a trusting relationship that respects client autonomy, while developing a common language based on the words, ideas, and values of the people we are trying to help. This is at the foundation of a pretreatment perspective that can guide the outreach counseling process. A pretreatment approach is particularly relevant for people who are either formerly or currently among the long-term homeless and highly vulnerable, and who are also reluctant to participate in treatment and/or recovery based options. Its applications are far reaching and useful with an array of hard to reach and underserved populations that are in dire need of additional resources and services. Pretreatment is defined (Levy, 2010) as an approach that enhances safety while promoting transition to housing (e.g. Housing First options), and/or treatment alternatives through client centered supportive interventions that develop goals and motivation to create positive change.

Five basic pretreatment principles (see Table 1 on p. 5) guide our work:

1. Promote Safety – Apply crisis intervention and harm reduction strategies

2. Relationship Formation – Promote trust via stages of engagement

3. Common Language Construction – Develop effective communication

4. Facilitate Change – Utilize Stages of Change Model and Motivational Interviewing techniques

5. Ecological Considerations – Support the process of transition and adaptation.

An outreach model based on a pretreatment philosophy affords us the opportunity to become both interpreters and bridge builders. It is critical that we provide clients with real options that can be fully considered, as opposed to pre-programmed choices that don't respect their individuality. Potential resources and services are therefore reinterpreted and reframed so the client can more fully consider these options and their potential impacts. This is the first major step toward building a bridge to needed resources and services, including housing and treatment options. It is a bridge consisting of a safe and trusting relationship between worker and client, as well as a common language that fosters a communication of shared words, ideas, and goals. Developing a client-centered relationship and providing essential community resources and services are the mutual goals of Homeless Outreach workers, Housing First staff and their clients. In essence, these are the central challenges that are shared by both the Homeless Outreach and Housing First communities.

This book explores not only the shared mission of Homeless Outreach and Housing First, but also highlights what we've learned. Basic truths are reinforced, like the importance of a client-centered relationship, the need for affordable housing, and the necessity of combining it with support services, and meaningful structure or activities that promote housing stabilization. It also explores both subtle and intricate aspects of helping by applying pretreatment principles of care. I draw upon my experiences doing Homeless Outreach, supervision, and instituting Housing First initiatives to illustrate the challenges, success stories and the many lessons learned. Case illustrations help to bring the material to life and can hopefully start an authentic conversation on how homelessness and our attempts to abate it are really a microcosm of the human condition. Beyond survival, we seek meaning and a greater sense of connection to our world. For people experiencing long-term homelessness, positive relationships and stable housing can be the pretreatment pathway toward achieving this reality, thereby reducing the risk of unforeseen trauma, serious injury, or premature death. The compelling narratives of Ronald, Lacey, Anthony, Julio, Janice and Michael demonstrate this, as well as provide a striking reminder of our own human frailty. I hope that these stories will help connect us to the plight of our homeless neighbors, and thereby serve as a call to action. Even though homelessness continues to take a heavy personal and societal toll, I remain optimistic that with proper guidance, dedication and advocacy, great things can and will be accomplished.

Table 1. Pretreatment Principles & Applications

Principle	Application
Promote Safety	• Engage with homeless individuals in order to reduce the risk of harm and enhance safety (e.g., provide blankets on cold night) • Stabilize acute symptoms via crisis intervention and utilize opportunity for further work.
Relationship Formation	• Attempt to engage with homeless people in a manner that promotes trust, safety & autonomy, while developing relevant goals • Stages include: Pre-Engagement, Engagement, Contracting.
Common Language Construction	• Attempt to understand a homeless person's world by learning the meaning of his or her gestures, words and actions • Promote mutual understanding & jointly define goals • Stages include: Understanding, Utilizing, and Bridging Language.
Facilitate & Support Change	• Prepare clients to achieve and maintain positive change by pointing out discrepancy; exploring ambivalence, reinforcing healthy behaviors & developing skills, as well as needed supports • Utilize Change Model & Motivational Interviewing Principles • Stages include: Pre-contemplation, Contemplation, Preparation, Action, Maintenance.
Cultural & Ecological Considerations	• Prepare and support homeless clients for successful transition and adaptation to new relationships, ideas, services, resources, treatment, and housing, etc.

Chapter 2 – Ronald's Narrative: The Original Housing First

> "Think of it this way, if you had valuable information... I mean something really valuable like the cure to a deadly disease. What would others do to bring you down?"
>
> – Ronald

Homeless Outreach and the Seeds of Housing First

During the autumn of 1992, before the term Housing First was widely used, I did outreach at a homeless shelter in Boston, Massachusetts*. This is not to say that outreach counselors did not periodically try to quickly house chronically homeless individuals with significant disabilities including untreated mental illness and addiction. We did, and the results were decidedly mixed. One could argue whether or not this was truly Housing First. After all, we didn't have prescribed housing stabilization services and the housing was not always subsidized or readily available. Instead, we simply did the best we could through our continued efforts to provide outreach and housing placement to those most in need. At the time, there was very little support and acceptance of this practice. We made the decision to prioritize housing out of our deep-seated concern for the most vulnerable among us. We grew tired of being told that our clients weren't ready to enter independent housing or didn't qualify for residential programs. People in dire need were turned away for not meeting eligibility requirements such as six months of continuous sobriety, or not matching the right diagnostic category. Other times, our clients adamantly refused to enter programs or participate in treatment and therefore remained home-

---

* An earlier version of Ronald's story appeared in *Homeless Outreach & Housing First: Lessons Learned* (Levy, 2011)

less and at risk to a variety of major health issues. Throughout the many years prior to formal Housing First initiatives, outreach workers across America took chances out of necessity.

This is the story of the original Housing First, as put forth by numerous outreach workers and expressed through Ronald's narrative: how the best ideas can arise from the midst of our day-to-day challenges. As with any good story, we are taken on a journey that divulges much more than the title implies.

Pre-engagement

Ronald, an African American male in his mid-thirties, sat at the dinner table seemingly oblivious to the bleak and noisy environment of the homeless shelter. He slowly rocked his head forward and backward with a close-eyed grin and an impish laugh. He did this repeatedly, like some odd kind of ritual, while simultaneously finishing his snack of potato chips. Most of the chips made it into his mouth, though several crumbs escaped onto his straggly unkempt beard. I casually walked over to his table and pulled up a chair. Ronald continued with his repetitive behavior and showed no real response to my close proximity. I could smell a sour odor of alcohol and noticed the evidence of a recent outside nap: his partially torn and faded gray tee shirt had some old blades of grass mixed with small brown crackly leaves clinging to it. A bit more disturbingly, a small black bug quickly sprinted across Ronald's forehead before returning to the confines of his curly black hair. Despite feeling a bit reticent, I gave my best efforts to greet him in a friendly and non-threatening manner. For a brief moment Ronald responded with a one-word acknowledgement, before quickly resuming his focus on his internal world. Although I felt a little stuck, squarely in the pre-engagement phase (see Table 2 on p. 26), I was hopeful of beginning a new and interesting relationship. Ronald was definitely aware of my presence, but rather than make an attempt at forced conversation, I felt the best strategy was to try again on a different day. I visited the shelter three nights a week to provide outreach-counseling services, so there were bound to be other opportunities.

Over the next two weeks, I approached Ron on three separate occasions. My first two attempts met a similar fate. Ronald appeared much more interested in upholding his privacy, and showed little or no interest in conversing with me. My third approach was guided by the anonymous Homeless Outreach adage:

"If you want to get to someone's head, begin with their feet." I offered Ronald a new pair of socks! This immediately got his attention. I introduced myself as a Homeless Outreach worker and asked Ronald if there was anything else he needed. Ronald smiled and said that he was all set, yet very appreciative for receiving the socks. I left him with a pamphlet that listed meals, shelters, clothes, and medical services for the immediate area. We successfully met the challenge of the pre-engagement stage (Levy, 1998, Levy 2000) by establishing an initial welcomed communication that promoted a sense of trust and safety.

Engagement and Contracting

During our next encounter, Ronald and I reviewed the pamphlet. He mentioned that he had been homeless for many years and already knew most of the area's service and resource options. He even cued me in on a meal program that was not listed. I thanked him for the information and promised to pass it on to others in need. At the end of our meeting, I quickly mentioned that we could see if he qualified for benefits ranging from food stamps to emergency assistance and Social Security. Ronald didn't say much, so I stated, "We could always talk about this or other ways of getting income at another time." Ron looked up and said, "That'd be fine." Though it wasn't very clear how he perceived my offer, further contact around assessing Ron's eligibility for benefits was a distinct possibility. At least our conversation ended with the expectation of further meetings. Our challenge, which is central to the engagement process (Levy, 1998, Levy 2000), was to form a mutually acceptable *ongoing* communication that promotes trust and respects individual autonomy, so that Ron could be empowered toward discussing and setting goals.

Approximately three days later, I approached Ronald at the shelter. He was once again sitting alone and rocking his body back and forth. He then slowly reached out his arm and appeared to pick up an imaginary small object (between his thumb and pointer finger) and proceeded to gently move it thru the air. I asked him what he was doing and he replied, "I am playing chess." I then asked him what piece had he moved and he responded in flawless chess language, "The white knight to queen-bishop's 3." Surprised and delighted by Ronald's apparent interest in chess, I asked if I could join him for the game's opening moves. We proceeded to play imaginary chess for two or three moves, at which point I had difficulty visualizing the position of the chess pieces on the board, though Ronald appeared enthralled. I then stated, "Perhaps one day I could bring in my chess set and we could play a game." Ronald smiled and nodded, while stating that he used to play chess on a regular basis. We both agreed that chess is a great way to stimulate the mind, and then I asked if he had any thoughts about my offer to look into benefits or other ways to establish an income. Ron now showed improved eye contact and in a very sincere voice said that he really appreciated my concern, but didn't want to be a bother. He also stated that he was currently focused on finding a place to live, though he did not indicate a need for my assistance. Ron now showed greater connection. He was more easily engaged in conversation and expressed an interest in finding a residence. Considering that I had not yet observed him talking with others, this level of engagement seemed significant. I thought about an immediate offer to fill out housing applications, but didn't want to push things too fast and thereby appear overly directive. Instead, I clearly stated that he was not at all a bother and reinforced that my work (defining roles) was centered on helping people to pursue their goals inclusive of affordable housing.

Afterward, I reflected on Ronald's world. He seemed to value his privacy and showed indications of considerable difficulty connecting with others. He came across as intelligent and exceedingly polite, while concerned about being a "bother" to others. His mental status reflected both substance abuse and mental health issues as evidenced by the smell of alcohol on his breath, as well as his level of isolation, talking to himself and his repetitive rocking behaviors. In addition, he was among the hardcore homeless, meaning that he had been homeless for a long period of time and it was not unusual for him to sleep outside. While there was a great deal I didn't know about Ronald's interests, strengths and difficulties, it was already clear to me that our continued engagement would remain tenuous unless we developed goals that could serve to motivate and invest Ron in our meetings. We were in need of a guiding purpose that could resonate well in his world, even if this differed from my initial inclination to help with applying for benefits or offering a treatment referral.

A couple of days later, I approached Ronald at the shelter and he greeted me with a boisterous voice and with a greater sense of confidence and control. His repetitive behaviors of rocking back and forth in isolation were gone. It was evident that this was at the expense of some very recent alcohol and possibly drug intake. He was inebriated and this helped him to be more forthright with his communication. I told Ron that he appeared less anxious and more outgoing and then directly asked, "Do you have any ideas as to why things are so different?" Ron smiled and said, "I recently took my medicine (slang for drugs)." I laughed knowingly and said, "You mean 'un-prescribed' medication!" Ron nodded in agreement before going on to share some of his frustrations over being homeless and impoverished. He reported having been homeless for at least five years and said that he really would like to get off the streets as quickly as possible. He explained that he didn't feel comfortable at the shelter or particularly safe when he slept outside. I reflected back. "It sounds like times are hard" and then mentioned that we could look for affordable housing options. Ronald pulled out of his back pocket a worn and crumpled flyer on local housing resources. Together we reviewed the flyer, much like our previous review of the pamphlet on meals and shelters, except this time he'd initiated the review. After several approaches and three follow up meetings, we were now on the cusp of contracting for services. Ron had clearly requested help with a housing search and we ended our meeting with a plan to apply for subsidized housing. My hope was that the goal of finding affordable housing would be a natural conduit toward exploring his need for income, as well as understanding the potential benefits of mental health and substance abuse treatment.

Contracting and Re-contracting

Ronald and I met again at the shelter to fill out some forms for subsidized housing. The shelter was incredibly noisy and several shelter guests were intoxicated and rambunctious. Ron was once again high and had difficulty focusing on our paperwork. Nevertheless, we made it through one housing application before losing gumption due to his lethargy and lack of focus. I asked, "Do you think your un-prescribed medication has something to do with your low energy level?" Ron was silent for several seconds before sharing his sense of desperation, "Living at this shelter makes it impossible for me! I needed something to calm my nerves!" I went on to explain, "Considering the wait for subsidized housing could take several months, you might want to think about a quicker, safer, and more private alternative to the shelter." We left off with the understanding that we would explore these possibilities, while filling out additional housing forms during our next meeting. He agreed to meet the following morning at my local downtown office, which would be considerably quieter than the shelter. Ron and I made some initial progress with the development of a common language. We focused on safety and privacy issues, as well as finding a mutually acceptable way to refer to his alcohol and drug use as "unprescribed medication." Ronald even shared some useful mental health terminology, when he referred to the need to calm his nerves. Another promising development was our agreement to meet at my office. This would afford us the opportunity to work on things earlier in the day away from the amped up shelter environment, and hopefully prior to his heavy drug and/or alcohol use.

I waited at my office for over an hour and Ron was a "no show." At around two in the afternoon I heard a gentle knock on my door. It was Ronald! He appeared a bit shaky, and very quiet… generally ill at ease. He presented as anxious and depressed, while being very apologetic for his lateness. I didn't smell any alcohol and could not tell if he was high, but wondered if I saw evidence of withdrawal. I picked up on the here and now and asked how it felt trying to get to our scheduled meeting. Ron expressed extreme difficulty with the task. He felt very anxious when traveling and was not comfortable entering unfamiliar buildings or riding in elevators. As he spoke, his body began to tremble and he appeared genuinely upset. I commented on how over our last two meetings he sometimes appeared less anxious and more outgoing, though clearly intoxicated. Ron turned his gaze away from me, while nodding in agreement.

I asked, "What are the main reasons for taking your unprescribed medication?" Ron insisted, "I take my meds to calm my nerves." I reflected back, "It sounds like you are using alcohol and possibly other drugs in an effort to reduce stress?" Ron once again nodded. I shared, "The difficulty with that strategy is that it's only a temporary fix. Not only does your anxiety come back, but also you're on a roller coaster of coming down and needing to take more to get back up." I then asked, "Does that sound accurate?" Ron replied, "It's a dilemma, but there are no easy answers when I feel this way." I said, "Maybe down the road we could figure out some other options." I then suggested that if Ron could get out of the chaotic environment of the shelter he may feel safer and more secure. Ron immediately agreed with this evident point, so I went on to discuss some local transitional settings that would be far quieter than the shelter. Ron did not respond immediately, so I added that if he wanted more information we could arrange a tour or that I would be happy to share more of the details. Ron politely reminded me that he preferred to focus on getting housed as soon as possible and didn't want to get sidetracked, so we completed two more housing applications. During this time, Ron shared that he was a non-combat veteran. This was important information because it entitled him to priority status for at least one or two project-based subsidies. Before departing, Ron and I agreed to meet again in an effort to fill out at least one more application, as well as to consider future income options so he could eventually pay rent. Our discussion of income in relation to a housing search seemed like a natural progression, and much less forced than my initial attempts of bringing up social security and welfare in a vacuum. We appeared to be on the right road now that housing was our main focus. At the same time, there was some initial success in framing a dilemma around Ron's anxiety level and his inclination to use alcohol and drugs. Similarly, this particular health issue would have more power and resonance if it could be framed in regard to future housing and income considerations.

The following day I saw Ron sitting and rocking in the waiting area of my office. He appeared oblivious to his surroundings as he laughed and muttered to himself. We immediately started on another housing form, despite my initial inclination to focus on his mental status and asking clinically relevant questions. This was a judgment call, but I thought that it was important to deal with the housing issue first, before bringing up other issues. Once the application was filled out, I asked if he had any thoughts on how to establish an income, so he could afford to pay rent. Ron shrugged his shoulders, looked down, and quietly said, "I've bothered you enough. There is no use continuing with this." I quickly replied, "Ron, through my work I've met many people who have felt like giving up, yet we've been able to secure income and housing. It may take a little time, but I know that we can do this!" Ron did not immediately respond. Instead he remained silent, while averting his eyes toward the floor. What Ron didn't know was that I was a bit taken aback by both his statement and his prolonged silence. I realized that this was part of Ron's pattern of withdrawing from things. Most likely it was his way of avoiding uncomfortable topics, which often resulted in him feeling stuck and helpless. My next response was an artful and supportive confrontation to his avoidance. I said, "We can definitely resolve the income issue. I just need your help in figuring out whether it makes sense to find a job or to apply for benefits... Can we figure that out together?" Ron looked up and nodded.

Contract Implementation – Preparation and Action Phases

Ron and I had now successfully contracted to work toward attaining an income and affordable housing. At our next meeting I highlighted that we already had five housing applications pending with priority status due to his history of military service. If we could establish an income, we would be well on our way. With that in mind, Ron agreed to partake in an assessment of his job history and his current ability to gain meaningful employment. It was clear to me that his mental status was greatly compromised and very likely to interfere with his ability to work. Yet, I really didn't know Ron's perspective. This was my opportunity to gauge Ron's level of insight. More importantly, our joint assessment would give me a window into Ron's world, as well as help us to develop a mutual understanding on how to best proceed.

We met for almost an hour. As I like to say, we finally had our session! Ron told his story. He shared that he came from a large family and grew up in Mattapan, MA. He had three brothers and two sisters and they were no longer in communication. He felt very close to his mother, but now that he was older he didn't want to be a bother to her. He did not want her to worry about his troubles. He'd never been close with his father. His mom and dad had separated when he was very young. His most salient childhood memories were of him being constantly teased by others and often beaten by his brothers or other neighborhood kids. He constantly lived in fear and was very anxious about what would happen to him. He graduated high school and attended a year of community college, before feeling overwhelmed, falling behind and dropping out. His work history consisted of approximately two years in the army, before he achieved an honorable discharge due to issues with stress. Afterward, he worked in various manual labor jobs such as factory work, with his longest job lasting 10 months. He rented a room from time to time and lived with a girlfriend for almost a year before they broke up. This led to his current episode of homelessness. He'd been homeless for at least 5 years and had occasionally done some day labor, but it had been at least 6 years since he'd held a steady job. He reported being a loner, because he felt safer that way.

I thanked Ron for being so forthright and reflected that it sounded like he'd been on a difficult road. Sensing a strong connection, I took a chance and said, "You've had to deal with a great deal of fear and anxiety with no easy answers. Perhaps we could talk a little more about what type of stress and anxiety you've experienced and how your habit of taking un-prescribed medications began?" This led to an extended discussion that took place over our next two meetings. Ron shared his difficulties with addiction. He specifically talked about having drunk too much since his early teen years, as well as smoking crack. He reported that his crack use had been particularly frequent about six months ago, but he had since slowed down. Ron also expressed his deep-seated anxiety and fear of others, his inability to deal with social situations, and his need to be alone. He described full blown symptoms of panic he had experienced since high school and prior to his drug and alcohol use. By the end of our session, we were in agreement to consider other ways of managing stress apart from alcohol and drug use. We also agreed that he would apply for Social Security benefits (SSI/SSDI), as well as Emergency Assistance funds from the Welfare Department. Fortunately, Ron already had a primary physician who could assist by signing off on the disability verification(s) needed to attain benefits. We made plans for a follow up meeting to finish filling out forms, as well as to consider other approaches for managing stress and anxiety. This was done, while highlighting that once Ron established an income we'd begin a round of phone calls to check on the status of his recently submitted housing applications.

I now understood that Ron valued his safety and was very conscious of his isolation from others. He presented with significant anxiety, as well as avoidant personality characteristics. This is consistent with a history of trauma. His mental status also showed evidence of a thought disorder, though he had never directly confirmed having any delusions or auditory hallucinations. Things were further complicated by his evident addiction to crack and alcohol. While I wanted to get him housed as soon as possible, I was concerned that his level of drug use and psychiatric symptoms would compromise his ability to stay housed and to feel safe with neighbors. The dilemma was that we were considering independent housing options, yet we lacked access to support services and Ron had not yet begun treatment. However, I was aware of a transitional housing program with supports that specialized with homelessness and co-occurring disorders of addiction and mental illness. Figuring that Ron was a good match for this program, I planned to bring this up at our next meeting. We had now developed a playground of common language. Ron was initially comfortable with the word "un-prescribed medication" and was now directly discussing drug and alcohol use inclusive of crack. He also expressed a solid vocabulary of mental health terminology such as "anxiety," "stress" and "fear." Finally, I knew that he valued safety, so I planned to frame my offer as a way to feel more secure and less fearful, while waiting for subsidized housing.

As the leaves turned from red and yellow to a uniform brown, we met again at my office and completed applications for income benefits. Upon completion, I asked Ron to consider meeting with folks at a local mental health clinic so he could get some relief from anxiety and stress. I highlighted that this would also help him to secure Social Security Income as quickly as possible. My offer resonated well in Ron's world, so he quickly agreed to the plan. Feeling a bit exuberant by my initial success, I explained to Ron that attaining a subsidized housing placement was most likely a few months away, and so he might feel safer waiting for housing in a more supportive and quieter environment such as a transitional housing program. Ron intuitively picked up on the word "program" and adamantly refused. He began pulling away before I could even begin to divulge that it consisted of specialized programming for dually diagnosed individuals. At that moment I realized, if we were going to get anywhere, we needed to try independent housing first.

Over the next two weeks Ron began receiving welfare money and completed an intake at a local mental health clinic that specialized in trauma and anxiety disorders. We began some initial work around strengthening his coping skills, as well as more freely discussing his addiction issues and its impact on his mental and physical health. Within this context, I once again brought up transitional housing with support services as an interim option. I carefully avoided the word "program," while explaining the different mental health and substance abuse services offered. Ronald listened intently before indicating that he appreciated the offer, but was not comfortable attending groups. He reaffirmed his need for help, but clearly stated that he was not ready to do more. Although I still wondered if he had a thought disorder and felt concerned about his addiction, I was happy to see him begin outpatient treatment. It took about three months, but we were now off and running with housing applications pending, a source of income established, and pertinent treatment.

Housing First

On a frigid late November morning, Ron received a letter from the local housing authority requesting an interview and instructing him to bring ID and proof of income. Ron had been offered subsidized housing! Ron appeared teary eyed and said that he was extremely grateful for all my help. He then looked down and said, "There is something that I should tell you. I'm not sure if you will believe me, but I don't feel right keeping it a secret any longer." He then looked up and said, "There's a reason why I've been homeless for so long." I replied, "You mean something different from what we've already discussed?" Nodding, Ronald continued, "Think of it this way, if you had valuable information... I mean something really valuable like the cure to a deadly disease. What would others do to bring you down?" Bewildered, yet calm, I replied, "What do you mean?" Ron went on to explain, "About five years ago I stumbled upon the cure for AIDS. I can't share too much, but believe me... it's a miraculous cure derived from pure sunlight. Now, certain individuals who have some sway with the churches and the police are not happy about this. They've dedicated multiple resources in an effort to silence me. They are involved in nefarious activities meant to bring me down and take away the cure!"

I made eye contact and responded, "Ron... I really appreciate how hard it must have been to share such personal details. I am truly taken aback by what you've been going through. My role is to help you to feel safe and to deal with the stress in your life, as well as support your transition to housing. What you shared is really helpful because it gives me a better understanding of your world and the day-to-day challenges that you face." Ron appreciated my response and the session ended with a much greater sense of connection than we'd had through our previous meetings. The progress we made toward housing played a pivotal role. It opened the door to a greater level of trust and sharing, while also alerting me to what appeared to be a fixed delusional system. Understanding

Ron's world, I was able to express, in a sensitive manner, the importance of us sharing at least some of this information with his therapist, so she could help him to manage his stress and anxiety in regard to these issues. I also added that this information may help him to qualify for social security benefits, so we might want to revise his application. In the meantime, he could continue to collect Emergency Assistance money from the department of welfare.

With the New Year rapidly approaching, it had finally happened. Ron not only moved into his own apartment, but he also qualified for social security benefits (SSI/SSDI)! While I was extremely excited to hear the news, this was not the end of our work but a new beginning. Some questions remained:

- Would Ron consistently pay his rent or would his money get spent on drugs or alcohol?

- Would he feel safe and secure in his new apartment or would he end up leaving due to paranoid delusions?

- Is it safe to move someone with severe mental illness and untreated substance abuse issues into an independent apartment?

Fortunately, Ron remained dedicated to our weekly office visits. Now that he had a safe place to sleep, shower, and shave, Ron looked like he had done a makeover, appearing well groomed and neatly dressed. Further, his recent sharing of his medical research and the plots to bring him down seemed therapeutic. Ron no longer felt alone in his fight for safety and freedom. This level of engagement and trust was critical because Ron could choose to end our relationship and thereby cut himself off from needed support at any time. All he had to do was not answer the door and stop attending appointments. This was independent housing and not part of a program that required ongoing apartment visits or participation in treatment. This was the original Housing First arduously sewn together by outreach workers. During our first meeting at his new residence, we discussed some of the challenges inherent to achieving a stable place to live. Ron clearly understood his responsibilities with paying rent and taking care of his apartment. We also discussed his level of comfort with neighbors and developed a safety or crisis plan in case he ran into any difficulties. Predictably, major difficulties ensued.

The following day, Ron showed up at my office and appeared

distraught. He handed me a letter he had just received from Social Security. It stated that he needed a payee and was not allowed to directly receive his funds. I had originally recommended this because establishing a payee guaranteed rent payment, while limiting the amount of money that could be spent on drugs and alcohol. Ron did not agree with this recommendation, but we were still able to make a plan on how to institute a payee and I promised to help him devise a budget that would include a weekly spending allotment. I also highlighted that we could get a doctor to sign off on his ability to manage his own funds, but that was not apt to succeed unless we addressed the level of his drug and alcohol intake. Ron left our meeting with a sense of ambivalence. Even though he was able to see the advantages of having a virtually guaranteed rent payment, he felt disrespected and infantilized. I doubt he left with any increased motivation to address substance abuse issues, but perhaps important seeds were planted for future conversations in regard to his addiction and how it limited his options. Thankfully, Ron agreed to meet again in order to devise a budget plan and to further support the transition to his new apartment. However, he soon became less receptive to home visits and much more protective of his privacy.

Over the next two months, Ron reported major problems with unwelcome houseguests and his mental status had significantly deteriorated. He still showed up regularly for our appointments, but he was often inebriated, as well as more withdrawn and depressed. Further, he was now willing to discuss his alcohol and drug intake in more detail, but unwilling to consider going to a detoxification facility, which he desperately needed. Ron stated that he could not imagine dealing with groups and being confined to a unit. His treatment team via the local mental health clinic had recently begun Ron on a trial of psychotropic medications. These meds were prescribed to help level out Ron's mood and to alleviate psychotic symptoms, but did little to reduce his social anxiety. Ron experienced these medications as a major step toward reducing stress and helping him to sleep through the night.

The treatment team understood the importance of addressing Ron's anxiety symptoms without prescribing addictive medications such as benzodiazepines (e.g., Valium). Therefore, an anti-depressant that had shown some effectiveness at reducing anxiety symptoms was under consideration. Ron also agreed to continue counseling sessions that focused on enhancing his coping skills, as well as developing cognitive-behavioral techniques for reducing stress. However well intended, the effectiveness of this treatment approach was severely hampered by Ron's continued dependence on crack and alcohol. Similarly, our efforts to transition him from homelessness to housing were about to hit a serious roadblock.

Almost three months had passed since Ron had moved into his apartment and our meetings had become much less frequent. Early one morning Ron arrived at my office, and with a sense of urgency asked to meet. He appeared a bit gaunt and was grasping a letter in his trembling hands. It was a letter of eviction for disturbing his neighbors and for illegal drug use. Ron then went on to express, with considerable shame and frustration, how out of control things had gotten. Over the past month his drug use had dramatically increased, and the people distributing the drugs began staying at his apartment throughout the day and sometimes overnight. When they were in his apartment, they would play loud music, get high and eat his food. He was afraid to share this with anyone due to the continued threats of retribution. If he kept the door locked and refused to let people in, they just kept on knocking throughout the night. Due to the continuous loud noise, his neighbors called the police. When the police arrived they cleared the apartment of unwelcomed guests, but also gave Ron a notice to appear in court for drug possession, which was not on his person, but nevertheless in his apartment. Fortunately, he was not immediately put in jail, but now had to respond to a court summons. Ron, who had successfully avoided the police and others for so long, was in a real fix. He could no longer "not be a bother" by simply avoiding others. He was now forced to confront things in court or lose his housing and go to jail.

Remarkably, in Ron's mind the unwelcomed houseguests and the police had conspired against him. He thought that they worked for a wider network of powerful people who were assigned to discredit him and his cure for AIDS, so pharmaceutical companies could continue to profit by selling drugs to chronically ill people. This resulted in Ron and me discussing ways to better assure his safety and how continued drug use left him confused, defenseless and an easy mark for others to target. The present context of a pending eviction interpreted through the lens of a paranoid delusion jibed well with his need to think clearly so he could better defend himself. In that moment Ron had connected to the discrepancy between his overindulgence on drugs and his ability to remain safe. Hoping to build some further motivation and gumption I stated, "Ron, if you want to keep your apartment and stay out of jail, then you need to prove that you are actively addressing these issues noted in the letter." What I recommended was for Ron to enter a detoxification facility that specialized in dual diagnosis issues followed by a step down or transitional program. I mentioned that I knew the staff at the detox and they would be sensitive to his level of anxiety. Ron was now contemplative, but wanted time to think things over. We planned to meet the next day.

The following morning, Ron showed up at my office uncharacteristically early and was carrying a small black backpack full of clothes. Before I could say a word, Ron said, "I am ready to go!" We then made arrangements to get him into a detoxification program for dually diagnosed individuals. Even though Ron struggled with his anxiety on a daily basis, he managed to stay 12 full days. He left the detoxification facility in time to attend his court hearing. Because this was Ron's first offense coupled with his recent completion of a detoxification program, the judge was convinced to continue the case for six months without a finding. The judge stated that Ron needed to report back to the court without any new charges, as well as clear evidence of sobriety. If Ron succeeded, then the charges would be dropped. Unfortunately the housing authority was not as sympathetic. They stated that Ron needed to leave the premises, or he would end up in housing court. Upon receiving this news, Ron took off and began drinking heavily for several days.

Approximately one week later I knocked on Ron's apartment door and he agreed to meet. He appeared depressed and close to tears. He was now at a crossroads where every decision carried the full weight of major life consequences. I said, "Ron, it's not too late to turn things around. We have the opportunity to get your court case dismissed!" Ron sadly replied, "What's the difference, if I am going to lose my housing." In an attempt to revive hope, I said, "If you were to voluntarily leave this apartment, we can apply for a future housing subsidy, but if you don't then we'll lose that opportunity. I know of transitional housing options that will help you gain sobriety, while addressing issues of stress and anxiety. Not only would you get away from people who have tormented you, but you could graduate from a transitional residential setting to independent housing placement." Ron appeared to be listening, as evidenced by his looking up and renewing eye contact. He then weakly said, "I guess we can give it a try." Reassuringly, I responded, "This'll look great in the eyes of the court and could qualify you for a new housing subsidy."

After our careful deliberation, Ron was willing to enter transitional residence for people with co-occurring disorders. This meant that he needed to once again enter a detoxification facility, because the transitional residence, which was relapse tolerant, required initial sobriety upon entrance. Ron now knew that he was capable of completing the detox and understood that his future housing and freedom were at stake. He therefore entered a detox facility and transitional residence without major objection. Interestingly enough, this was the same "program" that I had suggested many months prior. Back then, Ron did not have the motivation and I did not have the leverage to convince him otherwise.

Over time, our relationship grew and the words, ideas, and values associated with treatment were no longer foreign or threatening. Undoubtedly my willingness to house him first, rather than insist on residential treatment programs, played a central role in establishing a trusting relationship, as well as helping Ron to understand that I respected his autonomy. This provided a positive and safe relationship for jointly considering restricted options set forth by the courts and housing authority. Only this time, he wasn't alone and homeless. Together, we could face these difficulties with the hope of a better future. It was during these moments of crisis that important insights were reached and life-changing decisions were made within the confines of a safe and trusting relationship. A Housing First approach provided Ron with the opportunity to learn by doing and sometimes failing, as opposed to being indefinitely stuck or stymied. This approach gave him (maybe his first) reason to trust the systems that are set up, but so often fail, to help. After approximately ten months of working together, Ron entered a residential program with a new-found understanding of the importance of achieving sobriety, even if a true sense of recovery still eluded him.

Ron spent six challenging months at the transitional residence. We continued to meet weekly at my office with the goal of helping him to adjust, as well as to consider future housing options. For the most part, Ron maintained his sobriety, though he contemplated leaving the residence on several occasions due to his perceived mistreatment by staff. Upon Ron's request, I stepped in on more than one occasion to serve as a mediator. My role was to help Ron and the staff to better understand each other's worlds, language, and values. In the end, Ron not only completed the transitional residential program, but his court case was also dismissed. In addition he found a self-help group that he really liked at the local Social Club program (Clubhouse model) that served adults with major mental illnesses. Finally, Ron accepted a referral to the Department of Mental Health for case management services and was placed in permanent subsidized housing with ongoing support services. The support service consisted of monthly case coordination and a weekly home visit. Once community based supports were fully in place, Ron and I agreed to formally end our working relationship. We decided to celebrate all that had been accomplished with a game of chess. Ron was ecstatic to see me pull out a chess set from my bottom desk drawer. We spent the next hour discussing and playing chess. Ron won the match and left our meeting smiling from ear to ear.

Several months later, Ronald dropped by to say hello and thanked me for our successful journey. He then proudly showed me his first paycheck in almost five years. The Social Club had provided Ron with a job counselor who had helped him to find part-time employment that was allowable via social security (SSDI) regulations. Ron was now working as a messenger in downtown Boston, and resided in a subsidized apartment with support services. He also felt a real sense of belonging at the local Social Club. Truly amazed at all he had accomplished, I wished him well and grinned, knowing that there were valuable lessons learned by both of us.

Lessons Learned

This is one of many original Housing First narratives. During the 1980s I remember advocates chanting, "Housing is Treatment!" Prior to the current Housing First movement, outreach workers across the country undoubtedly tried its many variants. The following are the lessons learned as reflected in Ronald's Narrative, as well as from our multiple experiences with implementing a Housing First philosophy.

- The same principles of outreach counseling (pretreatment perspective) apply whether we are working with someone who is homeless or living in a Housing First apartment.

- Offering Housing First is consistent with the overarching and guiding tenet of outreach, which is to "meet the clients where they are at."

- Attach affordable housing resources directly to outreach teams in order to provide better and quicker access for homeless individuals.

- It is critical for outreach workers and/or case managers, who know the client best, to support transition into housing.

- On call and rapid response teams are needed for addressing client crisis issues (psychiatric, addiction, and medical) and housing crisis issues such as resolving major conflicts with neighbors, property destruction, and non-payment of rent.

- Establishing a good and effective communication with landlords is essential toward addressing housing issues and conflicts prior and/or during a housing crisis.

- Rapid re-housing is important toward ultimate success, but the new housing is not necessarily independent housing.

- Both affordable housing resources and support services are essential elements for promoting housing stabilization.

- Helping clients to develop meaningful structure to their daily activities is an important component to dealing with isolation, loneliness, and reducing the frequency of substance abuse (i.e., social club membership, supportive employment activities, participation with faith based or self-help groups, etc.).

- Case Management staff should support transitions to needed community resources and services, as well as facilitate coordination between the various systems serving clients.

Ultimately, the formation of a trusting relationship is central to our mission. It promotes safety and supports critical transitions to affordable housing, while developing goals and motivation to create positive change. Moreover, Prochaska & DiClemente's Stages of Change Model (1982) provides valuable guidance. When the worker first encountered Ron, he was already at a *preparation stage* for action in regard to getting housed, while *contemplative* of anxiety difficulties and *pre-contemplative* of his addiction issues. Therefore a Housing First approach coupled with some initial exploration of mental health concerns made more sense than demanding upfront sobriety or treatment compliance. After getting housed, the worker's artful confrontation on how Ron's addiction compromised his safety and housing security (highlight discrepancy and foster ambivalence) played a critical role toward Ron's decision to enter a detoxification facility and a residential program for dually diagnosed individuals. A trusting relationship and Housing First strategy set the table for the artful confrontation that facilitated Ron's movement (Stages of Change) from *contemplation* to the needed *action* of residential treatment for acute addiction and mental health issues.

Pioneers, such as Dr. Sam Tsemberis, Ph.D. (Executive Director of Pathways to Housing), have done much to research, formalize and popularize Housing First as an effective strategy toward ending homelessness among certain homeless subgroups. Housing First is not a panacea for homelessness and poverty. This is a complex issue that encompasses economic and social concerns such as high unemployment, low wages, and the availability of affordable housing stock. However, we do know that it is an effective way for serving homeless individuals who are most at risk. Those who are among the long term and episodically homeless, while suffering from major mental illnesses and other disabling conditions, are in dire need of quick access to housing with support services. I believe that most people understand or can be persuaded that Housing First is the right strategy to help this extremely vulnerable homeless subgroup. Our hope is to restore health and housing for people experiencing long-term homelessness, rather than restricting access based on predetermined eligibility criteria. A Housing First strategy is an important part of the solution. If we are to be successful in either ending or significantly reducing chronic homelessness, then we must not only have access to a wide range of affordable housing options, but also quality outreach and housing stabilization services that effectively apply pretreatment principles of care.

Many of the interventions listed in Table 2 (next page) are applicable to various phases (stages) of the outreach process, yet have particular relevance to the indicated phase.

Table 2. Stages of Engagement

Ecological Phase	Developmental Stage	Intervention
Pre-Engagement	Trust vs. Mistrust Issues of Safety	Observe, Identify potential client, Respect personal space, Assess safety, Attempt verbal & non-verbal communication, Offer essential need item, listen for client language, Establish initial communication, etc.
Engagement	Trust vs. Mistrust Issues of Dependency Boundary Issues	Communicate with empathy & authenticity, Learn client's language, Actively listen by reflecting client's words, ideas, and values, Identify & reinforce client strengths, Provide unconditional regard, Avoid power struggles Emphasize joining the resistance Introduce roles, begin & continue development of healthy boundaries Establish on-going communication, Identify current life stressors, etc.
Contracting	Autonomy vs. Shame Issues of Control Initiative vs. Guilt	Further define roles & boundaries Address shame by universalizing human frailty and reviewing client strengths, Negotiate reachable goals to alleviate life stressors, Explore client history about goals, Determine eligibility for resources & services regarding client interests, Further define shared objectives by utilizing client language, Review & reinforce current coping strategies, jointly consider housing options, etc.

Concepts from Germain and Gitterman's (1980) Life Model and Eric Erikson's (1968) Psychosocial Developmental Model influenced the formation of this table.

Chapter 3 – Moral, Fiscal, and Quality of Life Reasons for Ending Chronic Homelessness

> "Whenever you are in doubt... Recall the face of the poorest or the most helpless man that you have seen and ask yourself if the step you contemplate is going to be of any use to him. Will he gain anything by it? Will it restore him to a control over his own life and destiny?"
> – Mohandas K. Gandhi (1942)

Introduction

We pay a heavy price for long-term homelessness[*]. It is not only a societal ill that affects all of us, but also has a negative impact on the health and welfare of the many individuals experiencing chronic homelessness. Wasserman and Clair (2010) state, "...addressing homelessness is literally a matter of life and death, as it is associated with all sorts of health outcomes such as addiction, mental illness, chronic and acute disease, malnutrition and violence." For many years, while providing outreach-counseling services, I witnessed this on the streets and in the shelters of New York City, Boston, and Western Massachusetts. Unfortunately, it was not unusual to meet people living on the fringes of our society without any sense of hope or expectation for the comforts of a better life. Throughout the 1980s, 90s and much of the new millennium, the response to homelessness has been primarily geared toward helping people who are most ready to accept services and programming, as well as providing temporary shelter for those who could soon return to work. In the meantime, long-term homelessness has become an all too common and accepted reality. In fact, research has shown that on a yearly basis 2.3 - 3.5 million people are homeless (Burt and

---

[*] An earlier version of this chapter appeared in the monograph *Homeless Outreach & Housing First* ((Levy, 2011)

Aron, 2000). Further, as much as 20 percent of the homeless population (Kuhn and Culhane, 1998) are either among the long-term homeless, or have had multiple episodes of homelessness. This is at the core of the Department of Housing and Urban Development's (HUD) definition, which defines chronic homelessness (McKinney-Vento, 2002) as an individual with disability (addiction, mental or medical illness) who has been homeless for at least 12 consecutive months or has had at least 4 distinct episodes of homelessness within a three-year period.

While economic realities that include unemployment, under-employment, and lack of affordable housing are amid the initial causes that can lead to chronic homelessness, other significant variables consist of major mental illness and/or addiction, and other medical issues that compromise social and vocational functioning. In fact, many shelters that have prided themselves in becoming safe havens for the poor and less fortunate have also become default institutions for long-term homeless persons with acute and chronic health issues. Meanwhile, among the many myths is that people who experience chronic homelessness are unworkable or dis-interested in getting help, or simply prefer their homeless life style. Unfortunately, the costs of writing off a significant proportion of the homeless population have been staggering. Misguided homelessness policies have led to both moral and fiscal concerns, while the quality of life slowly deteriorates among the homeless themselves, as well as throughout our cities and towns.

Mortality, Health, and Moral Considerations

Somehow we have convinced ourselves that people who are long-term homeless with mental illness, addiction, and/or major medical conditions need to seek treatment prior to getting housed. In many instances we have turned this into a litmus test by declaring treatment as a prerequisite for residential placement. While this has motivated some people to begin needed treatment, others have refused treatment and have thus suffered dire consequences. The stark reality is that our attempts to avoid "enabling" have led to far too many deaths. While we wait for chronically homeless persons to hit bottom and request treatment, higher numbers continue to die. Dr. Hwang, Dr. O'Connell and colleagues (1998) studied the vulnerability of particular homeless subgroups and found that people who were unsheltered or living outside for at least 6 months were at high risk of death if they fell into any of the following categories:

- Triple diagnosis: mental illness, substance abuse, medical condition (tri-morbidity)
- 60 years of age or older
- History of frostbite, hypothermia, or trench foot
- At least 3 emergency room visits over the prior 3 months
- More than 3 emergency room visits or hospitalizations in a year
- Diagnosis of HIV/AIDS, liver or renal disease.

Over a five year period, 40% of the people who were among these categories died and the average age of death was 47 (O'Connell, 2005). It is equally clear that a high proportion (at least 46%) of homeless individuals sheltered and unsheltered suffer from chronic medical conditions ranging from arthritis, hernias and foot ulcers to liver, renal, and heart disease (Burt, et al., 1999). These health issues, as well as chronic mental illness and addiction, are only exacerbated by unsafe, substandard living conditions that lack basic access to food, clean clothes, sanitary bathroom facilities and a secure place to sleep. When one considers the impact of unstable and chaotic environments on health issues, it's hard to fathom why health care professionals and residential programs serving at risk homeless individuals have often prioritized compliance with treatment above housing placement (Levy, 2010, p. 15). It is a given that successful treatment is often dependent upon living conditions that promote, rather than diminish, health and safety.

After considering the serious ramifications of a treatment first, rather than a Housing First approach, one may conclude that it is a moral imperative to house vulnerable chronically homeless persons as quickly as possible, while continuing outreach and support services. It is important to keep in mind that housing is not an end in itself, but rather an opportunity to continue our efforts to build pathways to needed treatment services and community resources.

Financial Considerations

The cost of long-term homelessness impacts us on many fronts. Just consider that every day someone resides in a homeless shelter there is a cost for the bed and the staff needed to assure their safety. Surprisingly, the cost for a shelter bed in New York City can run as high as $19,800 per year (Culhane and Metraux, 2008). In addition, the longer someone is homeless, the more likely that person will experience untreated medical, mental health and addiction issues. This not only leads to periodic crises for police, EMTs and emergency room staff, but also results in multiple hospitalizations. In other words, long-term homelessness leads to acute medical, psychiatric and addiction issues being managed and treated via shelters, emergency rooms and inpatient facilities at an extremely high cost (Kuhn and Culhane, 1998).

Malcolm Gladwell (2006) wrote a compelling article in the *New Yorker* that tells the story of Million Dollar Murray. Murray consumed large amounts of alcohol, while living on the streets of Reno, Nevada. From time to time Murray would get sober, clean himself up and resume employment. However, without needed support services, he would relapse and end up back on the streets. Inevitably, Murray suffered a number of chronic and acute medical issues leading to multiple hospitalizations. The cost over a ten-year period added up to more than a million dollars! This price tag did not even factor in police, EMT, and other emergency services that were separate from the local hospital bill. The problem is that there is more than one Murray! There are actually a high number of unsheltered individuals going in and out of emergency rooms, detoxification facilities, and hospitals throughout our cities and towns. A five-year study of chronically homeless persons (O'Connell, et al., 2005) found that 119 street dwellers accounted for 18,384 emergency room visits and 871 medical hospitalizations. The average annual health care cost for individuals living on the street was $28,436 compared to $6,056 for individuals who were successfully placed in housing.

Fortunately, Housing First options comprised of affordable housing with support staff costs considerably less than the status quo. The expenditure for subsidized housing and support services ranges from $12,000 - $20,000 per year, as compared to our significantly higher price tag for inaction. While Housing First programs are no guarantee against relapse, there is a proven track record of significantly reducing medical costs and maintaining people in permanent housing (Home and Healthy for Good Report, 2010; Stefancic and Tsemberis, 2007). The financial case for providing housing with support services to at risk or vulnerable chronically homeless individuals is clear. In addition, advocates, policy makers and providers now realize that the same argument can be made for serving long-term homeless families. Overall, the evidence shows that housing with support services not only saves lives, but is also a financially wise practice.

Quality of Life Considerations

Arguably, it is basic things like good health, nutritious food, a secure home, livable income, and positive relationships that are among the ingredients of a better quality of life. Successful Homeless Outreach begins with the challenge of building a positive relationship and offering basic need items such as food and a warm blanket, as well as access to safe shelter and/or affordable housing. Unfortunately, chronic homelessness and the growing effects of poverty have had a negative impact on the quality of life throughout our society. In many places across our country, the poor and the rich live side by side with an ever-shrinking middle class. This is expressed quite vividly in the homeless realm. I have spent much time meeting people who are impoverished and without homes next to Boston's high end stores along Newbury St., or beside New York City's Upper West Side's cafes. The irony of such a meeting is shared by all of us. Popular transit terminals like NYC's Penn Station and Boston's South Station have become safe havens for the homeless, while commuters generally make efforts to avoid eye contact or any kind of human connection.

Even in smaller towns throughout Western MA, business owners register complaints of homeless individuals blocking their entryways and/or frightening away customers. Further, many cities and towns have struggled with how to respond to aggressive panhandling practices. Finally, it is not unusual for families to feel uncomfortable or unsafe visiting certain parks or playgrounds because a person experiencing long-term homelessness has taken up residence there. While it is true that homelessness may not be the main cause of these problems, it is understandable why many people feel inconvenienced or even threatened by their homeless neighbors. Though it is tempting to turn this into a dichotomy of us vs. them, it is clear that we are in this together. In fact, it is this type of dualistic thinking that has led to unsuccessful homelessness policies and flawed interventions. Ignoring people who are homeless, punishing them, or worse yet, treating them as second-class citizens will not resolve this thorny issue. Obviously, people without homes directly suffer the consequences including poor health and a degraded quality of life, but this is also a societal ill that affects us all. Therefore, we must find a way to address this on both individual and societal levels.

Effective Pretreatment Strategies

Homeless Outreach

Over time, the world of a person experiencing long-term homelessness gets more and more defined by meeting immediate needs such as finding food and shelter, staying warm, and may even include ongoing efforts to feed addiction, rather than continually searching for work and affordable housing. Anyone who has experienced long-term unemployment understands the internal struggle of maintaining hope when the prospects of success continually appear grim. Many people who experience long-term homelessness are hesitant to trust others and have found a sense of meaning that reflects their culture, individuality, and homeless circumstance, while upholding their personal values and need for freedom and safety. These survival strategies, meaning making, and clinging to strongly held beliefs and values, form an integral part of the adaptation to the traumatic experiences of homelessness.

The central challenge of outreach (see Table 3 on p. 37) is to develop a trusting relationship that respects the autonomy of the individual, as well as speaking a language that consists of shared words, ideas, and values (Levy, 2004). This is at the heart of a pretreatment approach, which is governed by the following cardinal rule: Meet clients where they are at! The relationship is the foundation of pretreatment work, while common language development is its main tool (Levy, 2010). It is from the safety of a trusting relationship and the development of a common language that it becomes possible to offer potential resources and services that resonate well in the world of the homeless person. Ironically, there is often a disconnect between the outreach worker and the very resources and services that their clients need most; namely income and affordable housing with support services.

Housing First

It is essential that we directly connect affordable housing and support service options to outreach teams and shelter staff, so that they can be readily available to persons experiencing chronic homelessness. If we really want to resolve long-term homelessness, we need to offer accessible, affordable housing alternatives with support services. This includes very broad-based eligibility criteria that are inclusive rather than exclusive. Housing First does not require that people partake in mental health, addiction or medical treatment; or that they achieve sobriety prior to being housed. The basic premise is that people should be housed as quickly as possible with support services that can help develop pathways and/or bridges to community resources, services and treatment. Housing First efforts supported by HUD funds began during the 1990s, with Safe Haven Programs that were designed to house at-risk unsheltered individuals suffering from severe mental illnesses. The Safe Haven Model is a low demand alternative based on harm reduction principles that provides 24/7 staffing support and welcomes residents who are not yet ready to partake in treatment. The Pathways to Housing program located in New York City is widely credited as the beginnings of the Housing First movement. During 1992, Dr. Sam Tsemberis designed this program and instituted a research component to formalize best practices. Since then, a variety of Housing First programs with different levels of support have been tried in many cities throughout the country including, but not limited to Philadelphia, Boston, New York City, Las Vegas, and Seattle. Multiple studies have confirmed successful outcomes such as better than 84% housing retention rates, as well as reducing overall health care costs (Common Ground, 2012; Home and Healthy for Good Report, 2010; Stefancic and Tsemberis, 2007). Housing First programs and their proven benefits are discussed at length in chapter 9.

Critical Response Team

A Critical Response Team (CRT) connects elements from both Homeless Outreach and Housing First approaches, while adding a systems-level response for those whose safety is deemed at highest risk and can no longer function within the homeless services network. This often targets vulnerable unsheltered individuals with major disabilities who either can't tolerate homeless shelter settings or for one reason or another are banned from entering shelters and/or other programs that help to assure their relative health and safety. The response teams also serve those who may be a good fit for Safe Havens or Housing First programs, but are unable to access beds due to lack of availability, or because they are assessed at too high of a safety risk to themselves or others, or due to their continual refusals to be placed in any of these alternative settings.

The mission of the team is to save lives by putting into action a response that will help reduce harm, while also providing the best opportunity to access needed housing and support services.

The Critical Response Team is composed of at least one outreach worker who is engaged with the client, along with representatives from a vast array of potential helping services from housing and support services to representatives from statewide services such as the Department of Mental Health, Veterans Affairs, and the Substance Abuse Bureau among others. A select group of these representatives are called to the table as needed to consult, as well as to consider potential *reasonable accommodation* strategies to help build pathways for the outreach worker and client to access needed resources and services. This includes, but is not limited to, lifting shelter bans, as well as utilizing respites, rest homes, and particular housing and support service programs by waiving requirements in regard to sobriety, criminal record, or treatment participation based on the client's current need, recent progress and/or openness to support services. Some of the most dire cases may require the team to consider a range of involuntary options from civil commitment to medical guardianship. We recently created this team in Western Massachusetts and were able to successfully house (with support services) some of our highest risk individuals who had no other options due to poor housing histories, current bans from services and resources, as well as not meeting certain eligibility standards.

Here is one example of our success with this model:

At our monthly housing meeting, a service provider announced an opening at a residence that provided support and treatment services for dually diagnosed folks who were chronically homeless. Eligible clients were also required to be in the preparation stage of the change model (not necessarily sober) for addressing mental health and substance abuse (MH/SA) issues and needed the approval of the local housing authority to qualify for a project-based housing subsidy. The program followed harm reduction principles and was therefore relapse tolerant. During the same meeting, an outreach worker referred a long-term unsheltered individual for a Housing First program, but we did not have any available openings. The participants at the housing meeting determined that this newly referred individual was at high risk of death or severe injury because he fit the vulnerability index category of tri-morbidity (co-occurring substance abuse, mental illness, and a chronic medical condition).

This concern, along with the fact that the client had been recently found unconscious on the street, led to a CRT referral, even though he was disinterested in treatment for co-occurring issues.

The CRT meeting consisted of our housing meeting coordinator, the client's outreach worker, and representatives from the program for dually diagnosed individuals and the local housing authority to consider this case for "reasonable accommodation." Through the assistance of CRT we managed to admit this high risk-vulnerable unsheltered individual with multiple medical concerns along with untreated MH/SA issues into a residential treatment program. He clearly was not in the preparation stage and had a past eviction that normally would have disqualified him from the attached housing subsidy. Fortunately, both the service and housing providers waived those requirements, based on the client's high risk level and the agreement that the outreach worker would provide ongoing services to supplement the program even after admission. The outreach worker, along with program staff, collaborated well and the client has shown notable improvement with attending medical appointments, accepting payee-ship, and upkeep of his apartment, while remaining housed for more than 1 year. This was accomplished via a residence and support service program that would have normally rejected his application.

Before referring someone to the Critical Response Team, it is important to develop an initial screening process to help determine which clients are at highest risk, and whether other standard interventions, services and resources had already been tried. I recommend developing a forum for consideration of housing and support services referrals, in conjunction with a CRT screening of the most at-risk cases. A good screening process helps to educate outreach workers and others about other viable options, protects the Critical Response Team from over-utilization, while reducing harm to vulnerable individuals without homes.

Conclusion

Pretreatment approaches consisting of Homeless Outreach services, Housing First initiatives, and Critical Response Teams are proven and effective strategies toward reducing the financial and moral costs of chronic homelessness. This is not meant to minimize the importance of homelessness policies and overall systemic strategies needed to address the development of jobs, employment programs, and affordable housing, as well as promoting access to an array of needed services and resources. In fact, in many regions across the country, continua of care and Homeless Service Networks have formed with plans to end chronic homelessness. In many places, important steps have already been taken to integrate current services and resources, while targeting future funds to address the need for affordable housing and support services (e.g., All Roads Lead Home – The Pioneer Valley's Plan to End Homelessness, 2008).

This chapter highlights moral, fiscal, and quality of life reasons for both continuing and spreading these important efforts. One of the great challenges that lies ahead is to successfully transition from a shelter-based system of care to one that emphasizes front end affordable housing options. However, we need to be careful that we don't rush to close shelters prematurely and thereby put people at undue risk. I am reminded of the pitfalls of the deinstitutionalization movement during the 1960s, when we rushed to close psychiatric hospitals, before having an adequate system of housing and support services in place. We don't want to make the same mistake in regard to homelessness policies. While Housing First is an important tool, it doesn't resolve the underlying economic issues and dynamics that cause homelessness. The emergency shelter system may need to play the critical role of keeping people safe for the foreseeable future. In the end, we all benefit from a society that has come to grips with the importance of eradicating chronic homelessness and its negative impacts. The goal of ending chronic homelessness is not only a fiscally sound policy that saves lives and provides a better quality of life for all of us, but it is also the right thing to do.

Table 3. Ten Guidelines for Outreach Counseling
(Pretreatment Perspective)

1. Meet clients (both literally and figuratively) where they are at!

2. The relationship is most important – Promote trust and respect autonomy

3. Develop a common language of shared words, ideas and values

4. Be goal centered – Join the person in setting goals that resonate well in his or her world

5. Mutually define or characterize particular difficulties to achieving goals and jointly develop strategies or plans

6. Carefully support transitions to new ideas, relationships (stages of engagement), environments (desensitization), resources, and treatment (bridge client language to treatment language)

7. Promote Safety via Harm Reduction strategies and Crisis Intervention techniques

8. Utilize crisis as an opportunity to promote positive change

9. Respect the process of change – understand its stages and relevant interventions

10. Understand the person's narrative and integrate a process of "meaning making" with movement toward positive change

Chapter 4 – Janice & Michael's Narrative: The Challenges of Helping Homeless Couples

> "We've had our disagreements, but he doesn't scare me. Besides, we've kept each other safe from all those bastards." – Janice
>
> "It just wouldn't be right to leave a woman alone in the woods. You just don't know how crazy it gets out here!" – Michael

New Beginnings

At the turn of the millennium I was filled with hope. Perhaps this would be the decade of inspired advocacy... much like the spirit (Civil Rights and Peace demonstrations) of the 1960s. After homelessness spun out of control during the 1980s, the 1990s saw the beginnings of the Housing First movement. The prospect of great gains was now palpable. In many respects this was a time of new possibilities. My family and I had just moved from the historic city of Boston and its suburbs to the scenic hills, valleys, and towns of Western Massachusetts. I felt re-invigorated and found new meaning in my work with homeless individuals and couples. I was no longer bound to the urban centers of NYC and Boston. My new job included outreach at the local parks, woods, and riverbanks, which was a nice change from city streets. Over time I began to work with folks at their campsites, and felt a sense of gratitude for being welcomed into their world. During the autumn of 2001, while settling into my new outreach position in Western MA, I received my first community call.

Pre-engagement

The town librarian told me that a homeless couple was living in the park adjacent to her work place. I quickly walked over and found a worn wooded path shaded by a variety of pine and poplar trees. I cautiously made my way down the trail and as the public library slowly disappeared from my view, I came upon the makings of a campsite. It was in evident disarray... Clothes were strewn over bushes, old containers and empty beer cans lay on the ground near a tent that was no longer quite upright. In addition, a deep rumbling noise emanated from the campsite. Moments later, a woman popped her head out of the lopsided tent and impatiently asked what I was doing. The low resonant sound continued, but I could now identify it as the snoring of her companion from inside the tent. I quickly responded, "I'm an outreach worker and was wondering if you or your partner needed any assistance with anything?" The woman, a white female in her 50s, shook her head and stated with notable agitation, "We're not looking for anyone to get into our business." I said, "Believe me, I respect your privacy. Just let me know if you need any camping gear, or some help with housing. My name is Jay and here's my card. I do outreach throughout Western MA, and just wanted to say hello." After a momentary pause, she took my card, and curtly stated that her name was Janice and that her boyfriend Michael was fast asleep, so it would be best to be on my way before he woke up. I just smiled and said, "Sorry to disturb you. Please let Mike know that I came by." I then turned around and began my retreat back toward the library. I figured that next time I would bring a needed item like some food or water in an attempt to engage a bit more, or perhaps I would be better off looking for them in town, so we could meet on neutral turf. At least I now knew what Janice looked like and wondered how well she got along with her partner.

Engagement

The following day I attended a community meal program and once again saw Janice, except this time she was sitting at a table conversing with her boyfriend, or should I say talking at him. Michael, a white male in his 50s, appeared to be heavily intoxicated and oblivious to what Janice was saying. I casually approached the table and said hello to both of them, before offering to shake Michael's hand. Michael took advantage of the opportunity by tightly squeezing until my fingers were red and numb. I quickly remarked, "You have a very firm and strong grip... I'd appreciate it if you would let go." Thankfully he abided by my wishes. This led to a brief conversation with Janice, while Michael remained silent, though a bit more attentive. I reminded Janice and made it clear to Michael that I was an outreach worker and would be happy to help them with things they needed such as blankets, socks, general camping supplies, or some help with accessing resources, which included filling out applications for housing, or applying for food stamps.

Janice turned to Mike and said, "This is the guy I was telling you about." I once again gave Janice my business card and told them that on most days they could find me right here at the meal program, so maybe we could connect on things down the road. Mike was silent, but Jan showed improved eye contact, while inquiring whether or not I could help Michael to get a benefit. Due to the level of Mike's evident intoxication and the fact that my hand was still aching, I was hesitant to begin asking Mike direct questions about his need for benefits. Instead, Janice and I left off with the understanding that in the future the three of us would meet to see if I could be of any assistance. Janice and I had successfully entered the engagement stage, while Michael came across as hesitant and not yet engaged. I left our meeting well aware of the fact that Michael had not uttered a word, and yet managed to communicate some hostility by tightly squeezing my hand during our handshake.

My challenge was to continue to build rapport with both of them, while being attentive to my own sense of safety. Therefore, follow up via a public meeting place like a meal program appeared to be a better option than doing outreach at their site. Fortunately, I saw them regularly at the meal program. Michael slowly warmed up to my presence as evidenced by his friendly greetings, though he remained on the quiet side. Janice was more than happy to fill in the silence by sharing a great deal of information about how they became homeless and their recent struggles to keep their camp site safe from intruders. They seemed particularly concerned about theft, because some other unsheltered homeless individuals had taken some of their belongings in the past. They also did not consider the local shelter as a viable alternative due to their firsthand experience of shelter staff getting into their business and the general lack of privacy. The key to Michael's acceptance seemed to be Janice's approval and her encouragement of my visits. After three meetings I had a better understanding of their story and concerns, albeit more from Janice's point of view.

Engagement, Crisis Intervention & Contracting

The next time I was at the meal program Janice looked upset and made a beeline toward me. Through her tears and in an alarmed voice she exclaimed, "We have to help Michael now! He fell in the woods and he's bleeding... Oh my God... What are we going to do?" I found out that he was back at the campsite, and quickly called 911. We made arrangements to meet an Emergency Medical Team by the library near the woods. I asked Jan to go back to Michael and assure him that help was on the way. I arrived at the campsite with the ambulance staff and found Mike lying on the damp ground with Jan holding his hand. Thankfully he was conscious, though he appeared extremely intoxicated and blood oozed from his forehead. I alerted Mike that I'd brought over some medical folks to make sure he was okay. Mike immediately said in a slurred voice that he was fine, but I was able to convince him to let the paramedics check him out. In the end, they patched him up and he was able with some assistance, to get safely back inside his tent. The medical team recommended an ambulance transport to the hospital to do some tests to rule out a concussion. Mike adamantly refused, but was thankful for their help. We left off with a follow up plan of my checking in with him the following morning, and with Janice's encouragement, Mike agreed to my outreach visit.

The next morning I arrived at the campsite on a beautiful fall day and Janice enthusiastically welcomed my arrival. She was happy to report that Michael was doing better. Nearby, Mike was sitting on the ground drinking a beer and munching on some crackers next to a small rock pile. I said to Jan, "This might be an opportunity for Mike to talk with me. He may be more receptive to my help if we meet privately." Jan was silent for a moment, so I added, "You and I can also meet alone, as well as sometimes together with Mike." She nodded, and I assured her that we would check in with one another right after my meeting with her boyfriend. Jan grabbed a pile of damp clothes and told me that she was heading out to a more sunlit location to hang their laundry.

I sat down next to Michael and asked him what he was planning to do with the rocks. He began talking about their need for a fire pit because the weather was beginning to get nippy. He then arose and pointed to the traced out perimeter of this important project. As he worked on constructing the fire pit I told him, "I'm relieved to see that you are doing better. Yesterday was a real scare for Jan and we got really worried, which was why I called for the EMT workers." Mike looked up and said, "You don't know how much I appreciate your concern. Nobody cares what happens to us out here, yet you've been coming out to make sure things are okay." I was very touched to hear Mike's gratitude. I responded, "Well, I think that your health is of utmost importance, and if you'd allow it, I'd like to help in other ways." Mike looked down at the ground and softly said, "There are many things that I'd like to see happen. It's been a long time since I worked at the sawmill and it has been years since I've collected unemployment. Janice and I have been struggling just to get by." To my surprise, Mike was now open to conversing and went on to share some significant aspects of his story including his life before homelessness, when he became homeless, and how he and Janice became a couple two years prior.

This was Mike's first real session with me and I learned the following: He worked at the sawmill for almost 15 years and felt forced out due to back pain and a constant sound of ringing in his ears. He reported that the work environment was extremely loud and claimed that he drank a great deal of beer just to deal with everything and everybody at the Mill. He recalled getting into a number of fist fights and getting knocked in the head on more than one occasion to the point of losing consciousness. When Mike was 25 years old, he was married for a short period of time. This resulted in a son who was now grown and lived in upstate New York. He hadn't seen him in many years, although they talked by telephone from time to time. We discussed yesterday's incident and the associated health risks in an effort to point out a discrepancy between Mike's current drinking habits and his ability to maintain his own health and safety. Unfortunately he showed no interest for inpatient detoxification due to his unwillingness to be apart from Janice.

Mike flatly stated, "It just wouldn't be right to leave a woman alone in the woods. You just don't know how crazy it gets out here!" However, he was interested in working on getting benefits (Food Stamps, Temporary Cash Benefits, Health Insurance, and possibly Social Security) so he could afford a place where both he and Janice could safely reside. I explained to Mike that I would need to meet with Janice separately, just like we were doing, in order to see what services and resources she might need and he nodded in agreement. As I left the meeting I was particularly struck by Michael's long work history, the level of his addiction, as well as his concern for safety. Little did I know that things were about to dramatically change.

Later that night, I bumped into Mike and Jan at the town green in front of the library. To my astonishment, Mike had a shiner with blood dripping from directly above his left eye. I exclaimed, "Mike... What happened?" I took out my first aid kit and gave him a sterile pad to apply pressure to his wound, while they both shared their traumatic story. Apparently, a local homeless man named Brian was rummaging through their stuff at the campsite and Mike caught him directly in the act. A conflict ensued and abruptly ended after Brian assaulted Michael with his cane. Once Mike fell to the ground Brian took off. Jan firmly stated, "That creep has a long history of taking our stuff, but he didn't get anything this time." Mike chimed in with an animated, yet slurred voice, "Yeah... He's got Sticky Fingers and I am gonna chop them off!" Together we chatted about going to the police to file charges and getting medical attention. Mike was adamant about avoiding the cops, but Janice convinced him to go to the local ER to get stitched up. Together, and with little complaint, they made their way to the hospital – arm and arm with a bag of their valued belongings hanging over Mike's shoulder. It all seemed a little too familiar as if they had gone this route before.

A bit later, I dropped by the ER due to a nagging concern that Mike might seek revenge and that the physical violence could easily spiral out of control. They both assured me that they were planning to once again pack up their site and move it to a more secluded area to avoid further conflict. We left off with the understanding that we would soon begin our work to secure enough income, so they could safely reside in an apartment away from all the craziness that home-lessness brings. These recent crises had borne fruit! My relationship with both Jan and Mike has grown stronger and more directed toward helping. I left the hospital feeling excited about establishing a clear goal, and in essence, a basic contract for services.

A couple of days later, Jan came to the meal program and was extremely distraught. She quickly approached me and said in a deeply concerned and troubled manner, "Mike is gone... I can't find him!" I calmly responded, "Jan., I am sure we'll find Mike. Let's go talk in private." Jan raised her voice with heightened frustration and said, "You don't understand! He doesn't know how to take care of himself. Without me, he's lost!"

As it turned, out Mike remained missing for several days. In the meantime, I was able to convince Jan that it would be safer if she stayed at the local shelter, rather than living alone outside. This was my chance to work with her individually. After a couple of days, Jan remained concerned about Michael's health and welfare, but was certainly less frantic. Once she settled into a regular shelter bed, we met on a couple of occasions and she elaborated on her story. Janice shared that she had no siblings and was primarily raised by her mother. She had no memory of her father, though her mom was briefly married to a man who was often cruel and violent. I also learned for the first time that Janice had been previously married and divorced. Janice reported an extensive history of abuse dating back to her childhood. Unfortunately she had a history of layered trauma consisting of childhood abuse by her step-dad and adult experiences of violence by her husband, followed by an array of traumatic experiences since becoming homeless. After Janice and her husband divorced, she moved in with her mother who shortly thereafter got unexpectedly ill and died from cancer. Jan had no current job and very little work history outside of some temporary employment in childcare, so she no longer had the means to independently support herself.

When you factored in her significant trauma history with the loss of her mother, and the lack of ongoing social supports, her ability to find and maintain work was severely hampered. This sadly resulted in her becoming homeless and she ended up staying at the local shelter where she met Michael. They both decided that the rules and expectations at the shelter were unbearable, so they began camping out whenever and wherever possible. Once they began living outdoors there were constant conflicts, threats and violence with Brian and a couple of other homeless guys who lived nearby. I took advantage of the topic to query if she had ever experienced any abuse from Michael. Janice laughed and said, "We've had our disagreements, but he doesn't scare me. Besides, we've kept each other safe from all those bastards." It appeared to me that day-to-day violence and living dangerously had long been the common thread of their relationship. In the midst of such turbulence it is difficult to make judgments of abuse when their everyday experiences were filled with safety risks that they have jointly faced. One thing was certain, I had not yet noticed any evidence of abuse or violence between them, but would continue to stay alert to that distinct possibility.

I purposely limited our discussions around the details of Jan's trauma and loss, because I didn't want her to re-experience the ill effects of such a troubled history. This was especially important considering her current homelessness and lack of support. However, I did take the opportunity to provide some education on the benefits of receiving counseling and support for these issues. I then said, "Jan... You are really good at taking care of Mike, but I get worried that you sometimes ignore your own needs. I could connect you to a counselor who would help you to get perspective on things including how to stay safe and take better care of yourself. I mean, you've been through a great deal, so having someone who really listens and responds to what you are dealing with can make a big difference." Jan replied, "Why can't you be my counselor?" I quickly stated, "Janice, I am your outreach counselor. We can work together on getting you safely situated... hopefully housed! But you could also benefit from working with someone who specializes with trauma. I know a therapist from the local clinic who could provide a great deal of help. Would you like to meet her?" Janice pondered this idea and said, "Let's first find out what happened to Michael, then I'll consider it."

I left our meeting feeling good about my connection with Janice and us being on the brink of contracting for additional services. At the same time I realized that I was a lone worker trying to aid a couple, which puts in motion a complex set of interpersonal dynamics. Ideally, an outreach team could split up and provide needed 1:1 support and counseling to each person as necessary. Even though I didn't have this direct option, I certainly could refer them to separate counselors via the local mental health clinic. My hope was to build a clinical team composed of myself and their counselors. Together, we could more effectively respond to crisis. I was also concerned about the extent of the abuse that Janice had suffered and whether it compromised her ability to focus on her own care and safety. To this end, if Janice were to begin meeting with a therapist to discuss trauma and co-dependency issues, it might help her to be more invested in herself, rather than being almost exclusively focused on Michael's well-being. One of the essential steps required to help make this happen would be to offer Janice help with applying for Emergency Aid, which included temporary cash assistance and food stamps, as well as health insurance via Medicaid. This would enable Jan to have some limited funds for travel expenses, as well as health insurance that her mental health and/or medical providers could bill. I was happy that Janice was willing to contemplate change, yet saddened by her story of significant loss and repeated trauma.

Re-Engagement & Re-Contracting

The next day I received a phone call from a social worker alerting me to Michael's whereabouts. Michael was inpatient at a hospital located several towns away. The worker explained that Michael gave her my business card and told stories about my visits to the campsite. She wanted me to know that those visits meant a great deal to Michael and he was wondering if I could visit him to provide some assistance with discharge plans. Embracing the opportunity, I made arrangements to meet with Michael and the social worker later that day. I realized that this would be a chance to meet with Michael while he was sober, and was very interested to hear his perspective on things. A couple of hours later, I arrived at the hospital and briefly met with the social worker. She shared that Mike had fallen and suffered a major concussion. He'd been extremely intoxicated, dehydrated, and may now be experiencing the aftereffects of a traumatic brain injury, though his memory had improved considerably. The hospital staff was not aware of Mike's baseline functioning prior to the fall, so they were hopeful that my visit with Michael would help to compare his current mental status and functioning to prior to the incident. The social worker agreed that it was a good idea for Michael and me to meet privately with the hope of arranging a group discharge meeting (Michael, myself, and the hospital social worker) for later that week.

When I walked into the room I was so stunned by Mike's presentation and demeanor that I hardly recognized him. He was showered, shaved and wearing clean clothes! He seemed happy to see me and immediately inquired as to how Janice was getting along. I assured him that she was now residing at the shelter to stay safe from the outside riffraff, and he gave an audible sigh of relief. Mike then responded, while looking down at the floor, "I feel so hopeless and I don't know what to tell her. His sense of shame was poignant. I explained, "Jan was worried about you, but of course the main thing is that you are okay. Do you know how or why you ended up in the hospital?" In that moment, Mike responded authentically, "I really don't remember much. They told me that I fell and hit my head. I had a major headache for a few days, and have been a bit dizzy, but it's not as bad as it was. For a little while I didn't know where I was." Then to my astonishment Michael burst into tears and said in a visceral manner, "Do you know that I have a granddaughter who is almost 3 years old and I've never met her!" Surprised by the significance of his statement, I said, "Why do you think that's the case?" He then went on to explain that he talked on and off with his son, but it wasn't cool to visit his granddaughter while intoxicated. I then said, "Mike... being away from the booze, you've had time to think and talking about your granddaughter is an important step toward finding a way to change, so that down the road she can be part of your life." Before the meeting ended, Mike and I made a deal. I promised to let Janice know that he was okay, and he agreed to meet with me again, but now we would focus on ways of staying sober and future discharge plans. This exemplified the emerging opportunities that crisis and stabilization can bring.

The same day, I returned to the shelter and immediately met with Janice to tell her that Michael had been found and was in relative good health. Janice was notably relieved and said, "Finally! Now I can get out of this God forsaken shelter and we can get back to our campsite." I reflected to myself that when dealing with couples, it often felt like there were several wild cards in the deck... a bit of unpredictability based on their whims, interpersonal dynamics, and set of circumstances that they both experience together and separately. This was an example of one of those challenges. Just as Mike gained a new sense of motivation to work on his sobriety so he could see his granddaughter, Jan began showing a renewed interest to return to the woods.

In an effort to try and head off this potential conflict, I explained to Janice that Mike got pretty seriously injured, so we needed to get a better sense of how stable his medical condition was before making any plans for them to resume living outside. She readily agreed that we could pay him a visit to get updated on his health. I then suggested that we should find out what the hospital social worker's recommendation in regard to his follow up care. Afterward, we discussed the importance of Jan's own self-care and how connecting with a counselor via the local mental health clinic would give her additional support, as well as accomplish an important first step toward qualifying for temporary cash assistance via the Welfare Department. We left off with the idea that perhaps she and Mike could do better by pooling their cash resources to get housed, rather than to plan living outside through the cold winter.

As I left the shelter, I further reflected on the long road to establishing a clear set of goals and wondered about the future prospects of helping both Mike and Janice. One of the interesting challenges when working with couples was how at any point their paths can diverge or merge. It was unclear whether or not Janice or Mike would support one another in trying new things. After all, I'd offered and attempted to facilitate change, while they had in many ways adapted to homelessness, trauma and loss. *It is remarkable to think that my offer of help can easily be seen as disruptive or unsettling to their survival routines.* At any point, either person may be interested in change, while the other may remain hesitant or disinterested. The challenge was to either engage both in a change process based on mutual objectives such as housing them together, or to motivate each individually to pursue a separate path. Thus far I had initially engaged with them simultaneously, but then offered to work on specific goals separately. This was done in part because I was attempting to clarify whether or not they were both invested in their relationship, while I respected their autonomy to make individual choices.

The next day Janice and I embarked on our journey to the hospital, but first we stopped off at the welfare office to apply for benefits. I promised to provide transportation contingent upon Jan also getting something positive done for herself. Afterward, we trekked over to the hospital. Jan and Mike had a teary reunion. Shortly thereafter Mike reported that he continued to experience some dizziness, headaches, and a constant ringing in his ears. To Jan's dismay the hospital social worker recommended a discharge to a rest home setting as a next step, so Mike could receive some follow up nursing care, while restricting his access to booze. This would allow Michael to safely recover from his apparent head injury, while remaining indoors. The CT (Computed Tomography) scan completed at the hospital did not pick up on substantial brain damage, but his mental status remained compromised, though this may have been more evident because his chronic symptoms were no longer masked by alcohol. A future MRI (Magnetic Resonance Imaging) and a full neuropsychological evaluation were recommended to further assess for brain injury, though this was unlikely to occur unless Mike first accomplished a significant period of sobriety. Together we discussed Mike's evident need for further help, as well as the pros and cons of a discharge to a local rest home. Even though Janice did not immediately embrace the idea, she warmed up to the fact that the rest home was within walking distance of the shelter. This gave her the ability to independently visit Michael as often as needed and would certainly give her a greater sense of control. Michael appeared ambivalent, but agreed to the idea based on the fact that this was not an involuntary placement, so he could always choose to leave the rest home at any time. Since the Emergency Assistance application via the Welfare Office had already been filed by the hospital social worker, this freed Michael to work with me to try and obtain Social Security (disability) benefits. Jan was happy that they could simultaneously qualify for cash assistance, and thereby have the opportunity to pool their resources to get a place. For the first time since I'd met them, Michael and Janice embraced an overall plan to exit homelessness.

The day before Thanksgiving, Michael moved to the rest home! Janice visited Mike each day and they both enjoyed a Thanksgiving dinner, compliments of the kitchen staff. The rest home had the smell and feel of an institution. The staff were nice enough, but the environment lacked personality. It was a rather depressed atmosphere, and its occupants were mainly elders. After about 1 week, it came as no surprise that Mike was itching to leave. Of course Janice was more than happy to provide the encouragement. The funny thing was that I understood their striving to leave, even though I knew that there were some important advantages to staying. Pretty soon, they could begin collecting benefits and then we could work on a housing plan. If Mike were to leave, I feared that they would quickly return to the woods. Mike would once again begin to drink and Jan would be re-entrenched as the guardian of their campsite. This was particularly troubling because winter was so near. Unfortunately, this was exactly what happened.

From afar it appeared that we were back to square one. After all, Janice and Michael had returned to their camp site in the woods. However, the relationship that we established was stronger than ever and we now had mutual goals to work on. In conjunction, and in support of their housing objective, both Mike and Jan had begun Temporary Cash Assistance Benefits through the local Welfare office. More impressively, they were willing to accept some follow up healthcare. Michael understood that he needed to meet with his primary doctor and was considering getting sober or at least reducing his alcohol intake, though he was not open to self-help groups or formal addiction treatment. Nevertheless, he was now willing to explore the impact of his alcohol abuse on others, and more than once had expressed his desire to be able to meet his granddaughter. He had clearly gone from being pre-contemplative to contemplative of a path toward positive change. Similarly, Janice had further considered the effects of trauma on her life and future decision making in regard to it compromising her own self interests. She was open to meeting with a therapist via the local mental health clinic and was now awaiting her first appointment. Neither Michael nor Janice seemed threatened by the fact that while they shared a joint goal to get housed, they also had separate goals in regard to needed healthcare and counseling. We were at a juncture where the pretreatment pathways to help and housing had been not only imagined, but now existed. Some more work needed to be done to find a suitable housing placement, but Janice, Michael and I were working partners in attaining this goal. Even though they had returned to the woods, we were at a point where the three of us could meet together and separately to discuss our strategies, plans, and future aspirations.

Even though Janice and Michael shared a goal of getting housed together and had made some notable progress, some significant barriers remained. After all, it was early December and every day brought colder weather, and thereby put them further at risk. Access to transitional housing programs for couples was virtually non-existent. Even if Mike could commit to sobriety and was willing to go to a substance abuse residential program, Janice would not meet the criteria. Similarly, if Janice was to get accepted to housing with support services for women with trauma issues, then Mike would not qualify. Even their access to homeless shelters was limited to only one or two choices because most shelters focused on either men or women, but not couples. Family shelters primarily served women with kids, or couples with children, but not couples without kids. One thing was perfectly clear: Janice and Michael were unwilling to consider being housed separately, not even for a short time period. The limited choices that remained for them included doubling up with others, or finding a cheap motel with affordable monthly rates, or, getting on subsidized housing lists and waiting a substantial time period with no guarantee of getting actually housed. Things were further complicated by the fact that Mike started drinking again, and now he had some welfare money (approximately $46 twice per month) to fund his habit and a reduced tolerance due to his recent sobriety. This meant that the first few times he drank, he got grossly intoxicated and was unable to function. This is a serious health risk that many people who relapse face directly after being discharged from hospitals or detoxification facilities. Especially, those discharged into homelessness and have little or no support may be susceptible to severe alcohol poisoning, while not getting the help that is required for assuring their safety. Luckily, I was able to get Michael over to the emergency room, so he could safely dry out. Of course, Janice was there to comfort him.

Crisis Intervention and Contract Implementation

Several hours later, I met with Mike at the emergency room and said, "It's not too late to turn things around, but it is up to you. Once you are stable, we could find a place to rent." Mike heard this and declared, "I want to stop drinking, but look at me... I'm too shaky, and I don't want to seize!" We immediately called several detoxification units, but there were no empty beds. In response, the emergency room staff offered Mike an inpatient bed, and he agreed to a hospital admission. Fortunately, Mike survived his renewed bouts of drinking and was once again willing to try sobriety, or at least reduce his alcohol intake. I encouraged this by flatly asking, "Can you begin to save some money for a place to stay, rather than spending it on booze?" Mike agreed to a preliminary budget plan of saving $20 per welfare check. In response, I agreed to renew our housing search and to look into accessing rental assistance. We immediately re-contracted around Michael's desire to get housed and in an effort to further enhance his motivation, I reminded him of his wish to see his granddaughter. Together we talked about the challenges of staying sober and his need for meaningful structure. Mike and Janice had attended AA meetings in the past and Janice was now more than willing to encourage his sobriety. This was in part due to her concern for his welfare. Janice had witnessed Mike's slow, yet continual deterioration and had been quite frightened during his last disappearance. She didn't want to lose him again and his health was clearly on the decline. Janice had also saved a few dollars and if we were to find a place to rent, their welfare checks would go up to a combined total of about $600 per month. In the end, this was another example of the well-practiced art of turning a present day crisis into a future opportunity for productive work. In this case, Michael presented with the need for immediate detoxification due to excessive drinking, severe intoxication and the fear of seizure. Within this context was the opportunity to further solidify and redefine the purpose of our relationship, connect Mike to inpatient treatment and outpatient self-help groups, as well as review and reinforce our housing plan.

Supporting Transitions: Easier Said than Done

By the New Year, I was able to make arrangements for Janice and Mike to move into a cheap motel with a monthly rate tailored to cost them most of their combined welfare checks. This came to $500 per month and left them with only $106 per month spending money and about $45 in food stamps. When one factors in Mike's propensity to drink, their lack of funds was not necessarily a concern. They also continued to attend a daily community meal, which provided them with free food, some daily structure, and much needed socialization. In exchange for our hard work to establish a new residence, they both promised to attend healthcare appointments and to work with me on a budgeting plan to assure payment of rent. The motel manager agreed to rent them a place because I was able to get a security deposit via the Salvation Army, and he valued the support services that I provided. Over the next 3 months, I visited Janice and Michael twice a week at their motel room. In time I was successful in helping them to qualify for Social Security benefits. Their combined income was now greater than $1000 per month. We also made inroads with Janice establishing a therapeutic connection with her counselor via the local mental health clinic.

Michael continued to drink and remained at high risk for liver disease. He was able to curtail his drinking intermittently, though not enough to actually visit his granddaughter. This remained some far-off ideal he could strive for, but could never quite reach. On the positive end, Mike sometimes attended AA meetings and success-fully met with his primary doctor. However, their motel room appeared increasingly cluttered, and there was evidence to suggest that Janice had a hoarding issue. It was very important to engage Janice in the process of determining what to donate, store, or trash. This needed to be done in a very sensitive manner because Janice showed an emotional connection to her growing collection of items and wouldn't tolerate a quick process of simply removing things without careful consideration. This was her stuff and she understandably wanted a sense of control over the threatening process of reducing the clutter. In response, my weekly visits focused on straightening out the hotel room with their active participation. This consisted of us removing trash, as well as trimming down their belongings. Specific interventions were utilized to define the livable space versus setting up shelves and allocated areas for storage items. Further, each visit ended with us jointly packing up some things to be moved to a local storage facility versus throwing away or donating less needed stuff. Michael and Janice now had enough money to pay a fee, so some personal items were sent over to a storage unit until they could get a larger place. This was more of a harm reduction approach to hoarding by removing clutter and reorganizing space in a sensitive manner.

Janice's rate of acquisition remained an issue for future intervention so it would not eventually threaten her tenancy. Her mental health counselor was apprised of this issue, and Janice was encouraged to share her challenges, thoughts, and feelings around removing and limiting future acquisition of items. In addition, I met with Mike and Janice around the first of the month so we could walk over to the bank and make arrangements for their rent to be paid. All in all this was an effective set of outreach based housing stabilization strategies that had a high degree of difficulty to maintain. Consistent visits, remaining sensitive to engagement issues, and hard work kept things going in a positive direction… not perfect, but under control. In this manner, my work had transformed from street outreach to housing support activities though the underlying principles of pretreatment remained the same.

As the last of the winter snow melted and the first crocuses began to bloom, Janice and Michael were offered a subsidized apartment by the local housing authority. They successfully managed the move to a new affordable place. Together we celebrated the fruits of our journey, though we knew full well that things were far from perfect. Michael continued to have episodes of drinking heavily, and his health worsened. Though he remained unreceptive to receiving substance abuse treatment, he frequently expressed his gratitude for having a home. He once said to me, "Through the years I've lost so much, but now I can rest. You just don't know how much I appreciate having a place I can truly call 'home'." Over the next nine months, we must have visited the emergency room on at least three separate occasions. Eventually, Mike paid the ultimate price. Within one year of being successfully housed, Michael died at a local hospital with Janice by his side. He was only 52 years old. Janice was heartbroken, but she remained connected with her therapist and together we (Janice, the therapist, and I) managed to pay tribute to Mike and the years that they'd spent "keeping the bastards at bay." They were survivalists and with Michael's death, Janice was now able to take better care of herself. Of course this wasn't the happy ending that we had hoped for and strived to achieve. Before his death, Michael found meaning in leaving homelessness behind, and afterward Janice remained housed, while finally getting help for the deep and layered trauma that she had experienced throughout her life.

Lessons Learned and Future Challenges

When you've invested the time and effort to really understand a person's world, it makes the loss all the more profound. Prior to his death, Michael knew that people cared about him and was very appreciative of our many attempts to help him. He died with a sense of dignity, as opposed to being isolated, alone, and homeless. There are no easy words to express the impact of losing a client, yet this is not an unusual phenomenon. Vicariously and in some ways directly, we experience a great deal of loss and trauma throughout our work. The importance of self-care, regular supervision meetings and the support of other outreach team members cannot be overstated. I am highlighting this point because this case illustration is one of a lone outreach worker taking on the difficult challenges of working with a couple. Even though it is not always possible, there are clear advantages to working as a team. An additional team member helps to assure one's safety, and allows the opportunity to gauge who forges the best relationship with whom. Also, it makes one less concerned about the dynamic of "triangulation." In other words, with a total of three people (one worker and the couple) there was always the potential for someone to feel ganged up on, jealous or left out. However with four people (two workers and the couple), each client could get their own worker, which reduces this risk. This provides the opportunity to simultaneously meet individually or jointly, but with an advantage of the two outreach workers providing each other with feedback and sharing ideas on how best to proceed. Unfortunately, I did not have the resource of another team member, so I had to be extra careful throughout the engagement process. My work with Janice and Michael began with joint meetings, because that was the best way to initially engage them.

However, I was quickly able to establish separate meetings without either of them feeling alarmed or evidently threatened. Once it was clear that they both were invested in safely living together, we resumed our joint meetings to focus on mutually agreed upon goals.

The challenges faced by couples without homes are multiple and complex, and so the efforts to help them are seldom straightforward. The couples we meet are usually adamant about staying together and as a result have limited options. Most shelters are exclusive in regard to gender and even shelters that serve both genders don't allow men and women to sleep in the same quarters. Another common difficulty is that the vast majority of residential programs that offer supports and/or treatment do not serve couples. Also, it is often the case that one person in the relationship may qualify, or is ready for one type of program or setting, while their partner may be ineligible, not ready, or perhaps qualify for something that is completely different. This is because many programs and resources are geared to serve unaccompanied adults or families with children and base their eligibility criteria on gender, diagnosis, functional level and income, among other considerations. Predictably, this results in many couples being ineligible, or not qualifying for the same things. Many therefore take their chances by living on the streets or in the woods, so they can remain together.

Other difficulties include, but are not limited to, both parties being strongly dependent upon one another for day to day survival and immediacy needs, while entrenched in a pattern of ongoing psychological, physical and/or sexual abuse that threatens their overall sense of safety and wellbeing. While it is most often the case that the male partner is the abuser and the woman's safety is clearly at risk, homeless couples sometimes challenge this stereotype. On more than one occasion, I've met women who were quite controlling and physically abusive to their male counterparts. Regardless of whether or not there is evidence of abuse, it is important to establish separate meetings with both parties as early as possible. This creates a forum for confidential sharing of information that includes allegations of abuse, critical safety planning activities, and the consideration of living apart and independent from one another. Even though the evidence of abuse between Michael and Janice was lacking, it was still important to give both of them some private counseling time to share their stories, challenges and aspirations without the other one being present. This allowed them to freely express themselves without direct or inadvertent influence by the other party. If evidence of abuse were to arise, then the primary focus would be to promote safety, which is one of the five guiding principles of a pretreatment approach. Throughout Massachusetts and within many other states, there is a network of safe shelters for women that focus on trauma issues and keep women protected from their abusers. Meeting separately would afford the opportunity to discuss this option and to help develop a safety plan to leave a violent situation. While we must remain vigilant in regard to potential abuse and/or unsafe situations, the reality remains that couples living outside and isolated from others are at an extreme high risk of danger from a variety of causes. A harm reduction approach sometimes dictates housing a couple where abuse is suspected but unreported, so that it can be further investigated and effective interventions can proceed, inclusive of an active police response. This is one of the primary reasons that you don't see many housing programs for homeless couples. There is a great deal of concern around safety issues and whether or not the couple would or should stay together.

Beyond the issues of safety, there is a bias toward serving more traditional dyads, such as a married man and woman, or a mother and child, or two siblings. Deep within the recesses of our minds are certain judgments that unfairly penalize alternative couples without homes, such as people from the LBGT (Lesbian, Gay, Bi-sexual, and Transsexual) community, or two unmarried individuals with significant disabilities. We too easily convince ourselves that alternative lifestyles present unacceptable risks, or that a non-traditional homeless couple would never stay together. When serving folks with major mental illnesses, we have generally cautioned them against their natural impulse to live together, and have too often threatened their tenancies over such proposals, as opposed to finding alternative living arrangements and support services. Our perceptions of uncertainty and risk have often led to inaction. Even within the world of Housing First programs, many homeless couples remain forgotten. Yet there remains a clear need for targeted resources, services, and Housing First alternatives for the select and disenfranchised group of couples experiencing long-term homelessness.

Chapter 5 – Making Meaning and the Art of Common Language Construction

"Despair is suffering without meaning."
– Dr. Viktor E. Frankl

The Springboard of Potentiality

We are meaning makers! This is an integral part of the human condition that social workers, counselors, and case managers have far too often ignored. Whether it is somewhat hidden or clearly communicated, our language reveals our individual sense of values, meaning and purpose. As outreach workers and Housing First staff, it is important that we both understand the worlds that our clients construct via their words and ideas, and also grasp what they find to be meaningful. Once we have a better understanding of what people value, we can speak directly to that sensibility and thereby form a trusting relationship built on a common language. Then, future choices and actions can be actively considered, so new pathways to healing can be formed. This is the springboard of potentiality!

Renowned social science authors Robert Kegan and Dr. Viktor E. Frankl applied this to their study and practice. Kegan, in his groundbreaking book, *The Evolving Self (1982),* brings us to new insights by applying Piaget's (1957) process of assimilation and accommodation to our continual development from childhood through adulthood. Kegan (1982, p.78) broadly views Piaget's process of assimilation as "fitting one's experience to one's present means of organizing reality," and accommodation as "reorganizing one's way of making meaning to take account of experience." He thereby demonstrates how our interpretations of reality, and by extension ourselves, as well as our relation to the environment are redefined as we resolve one developmental crisis after another. At every developmental stage, the world and self take on a new sense of meaning, and with it new possibilities for future action. As outreach counselors, the success of our work depends heavily on the worker and client developing a communication that fits well with the client's perspective and is consistent with his or her experiences. If our words and ideas are on target, they foster the process of assimilation and accommodation that can help set the stage for positive change.

Dr. Frankl is a holocaust survivor who wrote the seminal work *Man's Search for Meaning* (1985). He pioneered an approach to therapy that centers on the human need to interpret and find significance from our life experiences. In essence, Dr. Frankl's thesis is that the ability to derive meaning from the many challenges that life presents, including traumatic events, is essential toward promoting our mental health and full potential. A sense of purpose is a powerful way to organize our being and define the world in which we live, while motivating us toward future pursuits. Dr. Frankl's work, which was profoundly impacted by his captivity at a concentration camp, highlights the importance of deriving new interpretations of traumatic events. As Dr. Frankl (1985) states, "Despair is suffering without meaning." The more we are able to redefine traumatic experiences into something meaningful, the easier it is to gain a greater sense of mental health, balance, and purpose, while preserving our autonomy. As it turns out, many long-term homeless individuals who have experienced trauma and are living in harsh unsheltered environments have thrived by constructing worlds full of meaning.

Old Man Ray's Narrative Revisited

The following is an excerpt from my book *Homeless Narratives & Pretreatment Pathways* (Levy, 2010, pp. 7-8), which depicts the world of Old Man Ray (a World War II veteran). In many respects, Old Man Ray was my first field instructor as he demonstrated the interconnection between trauma, homelessness, and making meaning. So let's turn back the clock to the 1980s, when Ronald Reagan was president and homelessness was on the rise. I was a young social work graduate, and like so many before me, full of ideals and ready to take on the universe.

"During my first days of outreach, I was immediately puzzled by the deceptively simple task of helping an elderly homeless man who lived at New York City's Port Authority. He was a short, stocky white male of 67 years with a long white beard. His mobility was somewhat hampered, but he could move slowly by using a cane to get around to the shops throughout the building. He spent most of his time sitting on a milk-crate and observing the multitudes of people making their way to work and other activities, while quietly having a quick nip. You could count on him to be there on a daily basis along with the variety of shops, newsstands and commuters. He called himself Old Man Ray and had become a fixture at the Port Authority.

The first time I approached Old Man Ray, he surprised me with his outward sense of satisfaction and connection to his environment. In fact, while I was still transitioning to my role as an outreach worker, Ray had long been adapted to his life at the Port Authority. During our first meeting, he said to me, "I am the night watchman! If you want to know what goes on around here, all you got to do is ask." He then went on to ask how he could be of service to me. In my mind, he had immediately reversed the tables. My offer to help him did not resonate in his world and I left our meeting feeling a little stuck, yet excited about the challenges of outreach and what appeared to be the enigmatic world of homeless individuals. I was left with an important and at times the central question of outreach: *How do you help those who are clearly in need, yet communicate no need for help?"*

Whenever I revisit Ray's story, I am struck by the amazing ability of the human mind to adapt to threatening situations. Here was an isolated elderly man without a home, impoverished, and due to impaired mobility, forced to spend most of his days sitting on a milk-crate. Yet he managed to maintain his internal sense of control. Instead of being overwhelmed with loss due to homelessness, or being extraordinarily fearful of strangers in an unfamiliar setting, he found solace as the night watchman. When I offered assistance, he quickly set me straight. Ray explained that he knew everything there was to know about the Port Authority. He saw himself as akin to an information center and instead of accepting my help, he offered me assistance. In this manner, Old Man Ray made meaning out of homelessness, and thereby adapted to what could have been a harsh and unforgiving reality. He accomplished this by finding a sense of belonging and purpose, rather than being overwhelmed with fear and despair or as Dr. Frankl would say, "Suffering without meaning."

The initial goals of outreach and engagement were to form an ongoing productive communication between Ray and myself. This was complicated by the fact that we were viewing our interactions through the lens of different developmental stages. The juxtapositions of our ages and perceived roles were quite telling of the challenges that lay directly ahead. After all, I was fresh out of school, brash and armed with my knowledge of resources and clinical techniques. When I first encountered Ray, I saw a highly vulnerable homeless old man who was in dire need of help. However, Ray did not view himself as a victim. He saw himself as a wise elder and a proud World War II veteran. Consequently, he could not see how a youngster, who was wet behind the ears, could possibly provide any type of assistance. For our work to become successful, I would have to adjust. I needed to take an approach that incorporated Keegan's developmental considerations into my communications with Ray. Instead of acting like a teacher, it was far more productive for me to play the role of student. It was all too easy to forget that Ray was the expert on his world, but he reminded me by demanding respect. Instead of offering answers and alternatives to his homeless situation, I needed to listen to his stories and thereby begin to understand his perspective. Once I changed my stance to that of a young man accepting advice and learning from the stories of a wise elder, our relationship began to flourish. Our developmental interpretations and the roles that we played were now complementary, rather than being in perpetual conflict.

Ronald's Narrative Revisited

Ronald's Narrative (Chapter 2) also demonstrates the importance of integrating the client's perspective, sense of meaning, and purpose throughout our communications. This meant focusing on the central task of common language construction. When I first met Ron, his main goals were to survive day-to-day threats and to get housed as quickly as possible, rather than address addiction issues or enter any kind of treatment program. We therefore remained focused on a Housing First agenda, and Ron began to view me as a trusted confidant. Over time, Ron and I successfully formed a playground of common language to draw from, which included such phrases as 'taking un-prescribed medication' to represent his drug abuse and 'reducing stress,' which referred to mental health concerns. Our common language base slowly expanded to include more standard mental health and substance abuse terminology such as 'therapist,' 'anxiety,' 'depression' and 'crack.' It was clear that the word 'program' was not allowed on our playground because it represented a lack of personal control and therefore threatened Ron's sense of autonomy. However, Ron did embrace the idea of protecting himself from others and welcomed the word 'safety' into our lexicon. Shortly thereafter, he revealed his delusional belief that he had discovered the cure for AIDS. Unfortunately, Ron's grandiosity was paired with a paranoid delusion of conspiracy. He also believed that several authorities such as the police and the heads of drug companies were trying to stop him from sharing his lifesaving discovery.

If I wanted to be successful in helping Ron transition from homelessness and eventually access needed treatment, then I needed to appreciate the organizing force of his delusions. Ron's purpose and sense of meaning were derived from his belief system. Rather than simply diagnosing and medicating, which was not a real possibility at this juncture, I carefully developed a common language that did not conflict with his world. In fact, things were taken a step further by integrating his belief system into my choice of words and concepts to serve as an additional motivation for change. My intervention, which put a high value on our jointly shared concern for safety, asked him to consider the degree to which his drug use had interfered with his ability to keep himself safe from others. This approach empowered Ronald to contract for detoxification services, because he had realized that his illicit drug use and intoxication not only put his apartment at risk, but made him an easy target for others to seize upon. Substance abuse treatment now had a new meaning in his world. Instead of being a 'program' that threatened his autonomy, it became a doorway toward safety and future housing stability.

Common Language Construction

The stages of Common Language Construction guide us on our journey to better understand our clients' worlds and bridge their sense of meaning to the pragmatic and achievable goals of accessing housing and/or treatment for both acute and chronic health issues. Through the careful application of common language construction, we can uphold people's values and join with their aspirations, while avoiding the common pitfalls of making offerings that fit our agenda, but are counter to their interests. Ronald and Ray's stories (among others) show that our communications are most effective when they reverberate within the client's world.

Our goal is to be welcomed into the client's house of language. If what we express is too foreign or disagreeable to the people who we are trying to assist, then they will reject our help and/or misunderstand our intent. In that moment, the process of assimilation and accommodation is brought to a sudden halt and we lose the ability to connect in a meaningful manner. The responsibility lies primarily with the worker to speak the language that is most apt to register with the client (see Table 4 on p. 68).

This begins with listening, reflection, and basic observation. The first stage of common language construction is to *understand* the gestures, words, phrases, ideas, and ultimately the values of the people we serve (Levy, 2010; Levy, 2004). In this respect, we are trying to gain entrance to their house of language. Through listening and reflecting client terminology, as well as directly asking what words mean or what the person finds to be important (valuable), we can begin to build a mutually acceptable set of words, phrases, gestures and ideas to help foster our communication. This becomes our playground of language to draw from, when we need to reinvigorate conversation and/or reinterpret important issues so they are more accessible to the client.

The second stage is to *utilize* our agreed upon words, ideas and phrases to promote the engagement process and reframe workable goals (Contracting Stage of Engagement) in a manner that resonates well with the client (Levy, 2010; Levy, 2004). The third and final stage is to *bridge* the client's house of language via our mutually developed playground of language to better understand the terminology that other potential resources and services may use (Levy 2010; Levy, 2004). It is important for the discussion of these resources and services to flow from our clients' specific goals and interests. Whether it is mental health clinics, self-help groups, faith based services, or even promoting access to housing subsidies and disability benefits, it is advantageous to learn and speak the unique terminology that describes those systems. The key is in our ability to translate this terminology back into a language that our clients can readily hear and actively consider. Similarly, when advocating with service and resource providers, we try our best to convey the needs/wants and eligibility assessments of our clients in a way that is most apt to register with their houses of language.

This is a powerful way to support transitions to needed resources and services. In this manner, Ronald was effectively bridged to needed substance abuse services and housing, because I was able to make offerings that did not conflict with the organizing purpose of his paranoid delusions. I focused on 'safety' concerns, which were among a particular set of words, ideas and concepts that he could readily hear. If I was to simply offer Ron treatment services prior to understanding his house of language, without utilizing mutually acceptable terms, nor bridging our common language to include consideration of mental health and substance abuse terminology, then he surely would have rejected my help. In fact, when I failed to realize his sensitivity and attached meanings to the word 'program,' it significantly delayed the process of positive change. Once Ron was able to consider his limited options through the lens of a common language that was consistent with his interpretation of the world and within the context of a trusting relationship, pathways to healing and housing stability emerged for active consideration and ultimate action.

Emergence of New Pathways

> "There's an old analogy to a cup of tea. If you want to drink new tea you have to get rid of the old tea that's in your cup, otherwise your cup just overflows and you get a wet mess. It's very easy to spend your whole life swishing old tea around in your cup thinking it's great stuff because you've never really tried anything new, because you could never get it in, because the old stuff prevented its entry because you were so sure the old stuff was so good."
> – from *Lila: An Inquiry into Morals* (1991, p. 25)
> by Robert M. Pirsig

Pirsig's quote connects me to the challenge that many outreach workers face. We sometimes meet folks who are homeless, isolated, and often not asking for help. People experiencing long-term homelessness have adapted to their difficult situations over many months, if not many years. Some have become attached to the same old cup of tea regardless of its age and their inability to move things forward. This can easily result in the experience of "stuckness:" the expectation or perhaps the acceptance of the status quo, which is driven by lack of opportunity, isolation, and the same old ideas swishing around the psyche. It is the relationship with an outreach worker and a new environment, such as a Housing First apartment, that can bring a positive and fresh perspective that sets the table for change. The relationship is both the sweetener and the piping hot water that can be added to a stale cup of tea. It combats loneliness and offers new ideas for people without homes.

While it is true that a developmental or existential crisis may completely change someone's perspective (empty their cup), this kind of sudden change is not often seen. Much more often, long-term homelessness is paired with a slow deterioration of health and this feeling of "stuckness," while we continue to lack viable housing and support options. However, we can certainly help people to modify their perspective and redefine their options once they have experienced a trusting relationship that respects their sense of autonomy. The process of common language construction is our way of getting through people's defenses against the threat of change from what is comfortable and known. Through the process of common language construction, we assist the client's process of assimilation and accommodation of new vibrant ideas, which brings with it the possibility for positive change. In particular, our attempts at *bridging language* helps to uphold the meaning that people have found, while jointly exploring potential resources such as Housing First and treatment, which can now be integrated with their sense of values and purpose.

In addition, clients will go in and out of crisis when their normal ways of coping are no longer effective at providing balance and adaptation to their current environment or circumstance. It is during these critical time periods that a trusting relationship paired with a common language can be the doorway to consider new possibilities and action, as opposed to continued inaction and apathy. When this is done well, fresh ideas emerge and pathways to a better life can be envisioned and embraced. If outreach workers and Housing First staff do not practice the art of engagement and common language construction, they may experience their own form of "stuckness." This is manifested by their offering the same tired responses or what I like to call "program speak" to folks who have long ago refused to listen to such jabber. In other words, the outreach workers have fallen prey to the "same old cup of tea syndrome," and it would clearly benefit them and their work to add a pretreatment perspective. The next chapter, through an extensive case narrative, expands upon the importance of a client-centered relationship, common language construction, and crisis intervention, while also exploring the interconnection between trauma, loss, and homelessness.

The process of Common Language Construction is based on ideas and concepts drawn from phenomenology and Narrative Psychology. Heidegger's book entitled *On the Way to Language,* as well as Epston & White's selected papers (1989-1991) influenced the formation of the following table.

Table 4. Stages of Common Language Development

Stages	Goals & Interventions
Understand Language	• Attempt to understand a homeless person's world by learning the meaning of his or her gestures, words, values and actions. • Interventions include observing, listening, reflection, and directly asking what particular words and phrases mean, as well as learning what is important to the client.
Utilize Language	• Promote understanding by developing and using a mutually agreeable set of terms. Build, modify, and use gestures, words, and phrases from the playground of common language based on clients cues. • Interventions include utilizing common language to ask client questions, explore the outreach worker's role, verbalize client's aspirations, and jointly define goals.
Bridge Language	• Connect and integrate the common language developed between client and worker with other systems of language as defined by available services and resources (i.e., housing authorities, Social Security, medical services, mental health clinic, self-help groups, vocational programs, etc.). • Interventions include connecting resources and services directly to client's goals, reframing commonly used words and phrases by targeted resources and services to be consistent with the playground of language developed by worker-client. • Preparing for interviews via role play and accompanying the client may also be helpful. • Prepare intake personnel of needed resources and services for the language that the client speaks. If certain phrases or terms may trigger a negative reaction, reframe and redefine these terms whenever possible, or seek accommodation.

Chapter 6 – Lacey's Narrative: Trauma, Loss, and the Need for Safe Haven

> "The birds are innocent and peaceful creatures that
> can rise above the mischief." – Lacey

Trauma & Homelessness

I spent my first few years as an outreach clinician working at a women's homeless shelter*. With very few exceptions, women who were eventually willing to engage in my services, or actively sought my help, had a significant trauma history. This was often true regarding past childhood abuse, as well as recent physical and/or sexual abuse from significant others. In fact, research shows (Domestic Violence Resource Center, 2012) that one out of every four women experience domestic violence throughout their lifetime, and as many as 80% of women in prisons have been victims of sexual and physical abuse, as well as nearly 90% of alcoholic women (Jennings, 2004). When one further considers the relationship between trauma and homelessness, it is hardly surprising that many, if not most women who have ended up staying in such harsh environments as the prisons, shelters and streets have had traumatic experiences.

Trauma and homelessness are clearly interlocked. What one experiences in order to become homeless can be emotionally devastating. The lasting effects may or may not warrant the DSM diagnosis of Post-Traumatic Stress Disorder (PTSD), but its impact remains profound and enduring. Sub-groups among the chronically homeless have experienced trauma at different levels. In fact, it is not unusual to meet homeless persons who have experienced layered trauma from an array of traumatic events. Veterans account for at

---

*An earlier version of Lacey's story appeared in *Homeless Narratives & Pretreatment Pathways* (Levy, 2010)

least 13% of homeless adults in America (HUD AHAR, 2012, p. 19) and many have experienced combat trauma. While less frequent, it is not unusual to meet homeless men and women with foster care histories, who report profound physical and/or sexual trauma during their childhoods. Further, there are others who have sustained traumatic brain injury (TBI). This can cause major functional impairment, as well as significant psychological difficulty from the traumatic event that caused it. In addition, the high occurrence of substance abuse among homeless individuals and the associated lack of judgment and unstable relationships can result in the increased likelihood of witnessing or directly experiencing personal violence. This is especially true when you consider the unsafe living conditions homeless persons often endure. The numbers of people who are homeless and have experienced trauma are significant, and so it is vital that a trauma-informed approach is adopted and consistently utilized.

Judith Herman (1992, p.134) states,

> "The core experiences of psychological trauma are disempowerment and disconnection from others. Recovery is therefore based upon the empowerment of the survivor and the creation of new connections."

The initial phase of working with people who have experienced significant trauma is to help the individual to become focused on safety, rather than a retelling of the traumatic story (Herman, 1992, p. 155, Finkelstein, et al., 2004, p.1, Najavits, 2002). It is important for the client to develop appropriate supports and needed coping strategies, before focusing on more emotionally charged issues. Hopper and colleagues (2010) studied the literature of trauma-informed care from various experts, panels, researchers and workgroups. They have identified four basic tenets as follows:

- Trauma Education: Staff need to be trained about trauma issues and learn to integrate this understanding into their daily work
- Promote Safety: Build and promote both physical and emotional safety with trauma survivors by finding safer environments or enact needed environmental modifications, establish and clarify worker-client boundaries, develop supports and skills to address triggers, implement safety plans, crisis intervention, etc.

- Rebuild Control: Respect client autonomy by providing choice and promote a greater internal locus of control and needed supports in safer and more predictable environments, empower clients to actively promote self-care and recovery

- Strengths-based Work: Identify, reinforce, enhance, and develop client strengths, coping skills and strategies.

A pretreatment perspective with homeless individuals is primarily focused on promoting safety and stability, while supporting critical transitions to housing and future treatment options for a variety of concerns, including trauma-based issues. This is facilitated by establishing a trusting relationship that respects client autonomy, while carefully proceeding with common language construction. The clinician needs to be extremely aware of the client's sensitivity to specific words and concepts that may trigger past trauma(s) and/or very charged emotions, while empowering the client to maintain a sense of control throughout the counseling process. If a person with significant trauma history feels that their personal autonomy is threatened, they can reject a potential helping relationship and other needed services. Pretreatment principles of promoting safety, relationship formation and common language development, as well as facilitating positive change and supporting transitions (ecological considerations) reflect the tenets of trauma-informed care. The following is an illustration of how to apply these pretreatment principles and basic tenets of trauma-informed care in an integrated fashion.

Pre-engagement and Engagement Phases

I met Lacey on a sunny autumn day. She was sitting on a park bench across from the public library located in Westfield, MA. Lacey carefully tore the bread crust from her sandwich in order to feed a small gathering of pigeons and sparrows. I was doing one of my many rounds of street outreach and was immediately struck by her demeanor. She was an attractive, 35-year-old Caucasian woman who sat with her back completely straight and stiff. Her posture looked a little too good, while she studied her surroundings with quick piercing glances. Next to her was a backpack with two shopping bags. I tried to approach her to say hello, as a prelude to offering services, but she quickly got up, grabbed her bags and rapidly walked away. At least I had identified a potential client, so I jotted down her description and location, while remaining hopeful of a future meeting.

Approximately one week later, at a local meal program, I observed Lacey sitting up straight and alone while eating her dinner. I approached her and introduced myself as an outreach worker who served the town of Westfield. I explained my role as a counselor who connects folks with needed services and resources. Lacey remained relatively quiet, while providing me with some confirmation by nodding her head and exhibiting good eye contact. Although we didn't talk much, I offered and she accepted my business card. Several days later, I once again saw Lacey at the park feeding the birds. This time she was more accepting of my presence, so I asked, "What interests you about the birds?" She spoke about their intrinsic beauty and the different types she had encountered, as well as how gracefully they moved. I commented, "Unlike the birds, it must be difficult for you to move around town with all those bags."

Lacey explained that she carried all her stuff because she often slept outside, but sometimes she "couch surfed." She went on to state that staying with others could be difficult, so she preferred going it alone. Lacey said, "I prefer animals to people, because my experiences have consistently shown that people can't be trusted." Lacey went on to share her yearnings for peace and privacy, and then reflected, "The birds are innocent and peaceful creatures that can rise above the mischief." In an attempt to connect with her yearnings and concrete needs, I mentioned the availability of the local shelter, and presented the women's dorm (at the local shelter) as a relatively quiet and stable place with secure storage lockers. Although Lacey appeared hesitant to actively consider this, we left off with the understanding that she could tour the shelter at some future time to see if it would be a viable option.

Contracting Phase, Promoting Safety and Crisis Intervention

The next time I saw Lacey, she was very tearful and appeared distraught, with heightened anxiety and agitation. She had tried to stay overnight with a male friend, but he kicked her out for not agreeing to have sex with him. Afterward, Lacey spent most of the night roaming around the streets of Westfield. I immediately reflected that she was courageous to stand by her values even though it meant being without a place to stay. This crisis provided the opportunity to frame the shelter as a safe alternative, so I suggested that we take a tour of the women's dorm to see if it would interest her. Despite feeling a bit shaky, Lacey agreed, and we walked over to the shelter. This gave us some extended time to further engage, and I oriented her to the shelter by describing how the women's dorm was developed for the stated purpose of providing women with alternatives to living outside or with others who are abusive or violent. Lacey shared that she had experienced abuse on several occasions in her life, including when she'd lived at a foster home, and by various male acquaintances throughout her adult life. She further reflected, "There were times when I felt so alone and helpless that I resorted to cutting my wrists." Lacey then showed me some past cuts and well healed scars along her wrists and forearms. I thanked Lacey for sharing some of her history and said that the current goal was to provide her with needed support and a place to live. I also gently reminded her that she had just gone through a great deal, and so we wouldn't want to compound her difficulties by reflecting too deeply on past traumatic events. The current focus was on her safety, and for us to address whatever we could to assure her present stability.

The tour of the shelter went well. The shelter staff invited Lacey to stay and she accepted. Immediately thereafter, Lacey and I sat down to jointly re-evaluate her level of safety. She reported feeling much improved and more hopeful now that she had a stable and secure place to stay. I provided her with the phone number to the psychiatric crisis team (24/7 availability) in case she had a recurrence of feeling unsafe or suicidal. Lacey moved into the women's dorm that same night.

Lacey stayed at the shelter for three full days before returning to the streets of Westfield. The shelter staff alerted me to her sudden departure and I found her sitting in front of the library uncontrollably sobbing. After about ten minutes with a mixture of support and gentle urging, Lacey was able to calm down enough to tell me why she had left the shelter. She shared an array of specific complaints ranging from the other homeless women touching her things and moving her bags, to the incompetence of shelter staff. She clearly felt mistreated and it was very difficult to sort out legitimate complaints from transference-based issues due to past abusive relationships. It is possible that unresolved traumatic experiences that had occurred during childhood years could result in an active mistrust and suspicion of others. Regardless, and more importantly,

Lacey had made her mind up never to return to the shelter, and felt very justified.

My challenge was to effectively remain engaged with Lacey, while addressing short-term safety issues such as where she could stay that night. It was now evident that the shelter was far too stimulating, and was bound to trigger past traumas and overwhelming emotions. During our extended outreach-counseling session, Lacey reviewed the current difficulties of living at the shelter, as well as how her past abuse history impacted her ability to deal with the interpersonal challenges and conflicts that occurred there. Lacey stated, "It is hard enough for me to trust and develop a good comfort level with a single roommate, let alone with several unknown people at a shelter." I reflected back, "Anyone who had gone through your history of pain and trauma would have difficulty feeling safe at the shelter." Together, we learned that better preparation, improved coping strategies, and a more suitable environment with supports, as well as having access to privacy were essential ingredients toward promoting Lacey's stability. Fortunately, this fit the description of a local safe haven program. Lacey appeared to be eligible for this program due to exhibiting some trauma-based symptoms, difficulties in utilizing the generic shelters, and her propensity for residing outside. However, before I could offer this option, Lacey abruptly ended our meeting, so she could safely (prior to dark) get over to her unsheltered site located in the woods. As she departed, we managed to make plans on the fly for a follow-up meeting at the local park across from the library.

I arrived at the park with updated information on the local safe haven program, and all I saw was some pigeons and sparrows milling around an empty park bench. Lacey was a no show! Nevertheless, I expected to have the opportunity to re-engage with her at the local meal program. Unfortunately, she was not at the meal program either. Over the next two weeks I was unable to locate Lacey, and I was left wondering whether or not she was all right.

It was now late October and the New England morning air had a winter bite to it. I began my early morning outreach rounds, and there was Lacey sitting on a park bench hunched over and crying. Her well-corrected posture was gone and it was immediately evident that she was experiencing another crisis. I was relieved to have finally found her, but concerned about her mental health. Also, I was hopeful that this would present the opportunity to address safety issues and eventual placement into affordable housing with support services. Lacey told me that she'd spent one night outside, before hooking up with an old boyfriend. They got along fine as long as she had the money from her Social Security Income (SSI) check to purchase crack and beer. Once her money ran out, she was quickly kicked to the curb. Lacey declared, "I'm tired of being used!" Her eyes welled up with tears and she once again began to weep. I calmly shared my sorrow for her pain and suffering, then asked, "Is there anything I can do to help?" I wanted to say that she could chalk it up as a hard life lesson, but feared that the timing wasn't right. It was better to wait until she was more stable, and more in tune with taking action to help herself.

Lacey went on to express that she didn't want to live this way and would be better off dead. She then screamed, "I can't do this anymore!" Although Lacey didn't share a plan to commit suicide, I directly inquired and her response was unclear, if not elusive. Considering Lacey's sudden return to homelessness, lack of supports, and evidence of scarring on her arms from a past attempt, I was justifiably concerned. I therefore called the local crisis team and made arrangements for a voluntary evaluation. I told Lacey that her well-being was of utmost importance and that we needed to visit a crisis counselor. I also said that the crisis team might be able to help us find her a safe place to stay overnight. I carefully used the words "we" and "us" in order to promote a sense of joining around a difficult situation. I realized that there was a risk of her rejecting my offer, but her mental status did not appear to warrant setting up an involuntary evaluation via the crisis team. Utilizing the technique of "joining," and communicating an overall sense of caring matched with a potential place to stay, made it more likely that she would seriously consider my offer.

Actually, I was fairly doubtful that Lacey required an inpatient stay, or even a detoxification from cocaine or alcohol. It only took a few minutes for her to become more responsive and engaged with our conversation, and she reported that the high intensity of her drug and alcohol use had been for a very limited time period. However, I realized that the crisis team could provide the opportunity for a referral and placement into a Mental Health Respite bed. The Mental Health Respite program is a voluntary short-term facility where people can reside while accessing treatment services to promote stabilization. Further, this setting could help prepare her for a referral to the local Safe Haven Program. Thankfully, Lacey accepted my offer to meet with the crisis team.

Lacey and I met the crisis clinician. We determined that neither a psychiatric inpatient placement nor a detoxification facility were necessary. Lacey showed no evident signs of withdrawal and was responding well to our support. In addition, we agreed that a Mental Health Respite stay would help Lacey to reduce stress, begin needed psychotropic medications, as well as provide time for her to consider a Safe Haven placement. Lacey was offered and voluntarily accepted placement at the Mental Health Respite Program.

The next day, Lacey and I met at the Respite Program, and she shared her history, which included many incidents of abuse, childhood foster care and extended homelessness as an adult. Her only permanent housing consisted of living with boyfriends and short-term rooming house placements. She'd had no contact with any family members since childhood, and during her teen years she gave birth to a baby, which was quickly turned over to foster care. Though we did not dwell for long on the loss of her child, the emotional resonance in her voice spoke volumes. Together, we reflected on how she'd lacked, through no fault of her own, a sense of security and well-being throughout her childhood and adult years. We then discussed the importance of finding a safe and stable place to live, so she could work on these critical issues. Lacey liked this idea, so I let her know about a current opening at a local Safe Haven Program. I explained that the Safe Haven Program is much smaller, and far less stimulating than a homeless shelter. It is staffed with counselors, and everyone living at the program has their own room. The Safe Haven program was a much better fit for Lacey's needs, as opposed to the homeless shelter, because it provided increased privacy, with a greater level of staff support. Lacey wanted to think things over, so we made an appointment for the next day.

Re-contracting, Promoting Self-Care and Ongoing Work Phase

The following afternoon, I saw Lacey sitting upright and calmly sketching her surroundings at the Respite. She told me that she enjoyed the serenity of the Mental Health Respite program and felt safe there. We spoke about her interests in the arts and she proudly shared that she'd once taken a college course in literature and enjoyed reading Shakespeare. I commented that her interests in the arts didn't surprise me, because she seemed like a sensitive soul. I asked her whether she was aware of how her sensitivity could be a tremendous strength. Lacey carefully thought about this and then responded, "Sometimes I get overwhelmed by my emotions, but I also have the ability to appreciate things." I answered, "Yes, the birds and other things that you've drawn show a real appreciation of their beauty." Lacey nodded in agreement, adding that she really enjoyed interacting with the birds and sketching their movements. We concluded that, much like the characters from Shakespeare's plays, sometimes a significant strength could also become a considerable vulnerability. Together, we came up with a plan on how to manage emotional vulnerability, as well as the intensity of emotions experienced, by applying her interests and talents toward self-care. This was an effective intervention of highlighting Lacey's considerable strengths, while simultaneously bridging our playground of language to the world of clinical care. Specifically, this meant developing a list of calming strategies such as feeding the birds, reading and sketching. Lacey could apply these different ways of coping upon identification of stressful situations, environmental triggers, or intense feelings, as well as continue to take her newly prescribed medications to improve sleep and reduce anxiety.

Further, I highlighted that she had already taken steps toward improved self-care by choosing to stay at the Respite Program, which is a low stress environment with good supports. This intervention reinforced the importance of safety, while upholding her sense of autonomy. I then asked Lacey to consider where she would like to reside next. We reviewed potential options that included returning to the shelter, living outside and/or couch surfing, versus trying a trial run at the local Safe Haven. Lacey was interested in hearing more details about the Safe Haven, so I explained that it was a voluntary program. I highlighted that if she was unhappy there, she could always choose a different option. We also discussed how the Mental Health Respite was similar to the Safe Haven in that they were both relatively quiet and calm in comparison to the shelter. Lacey understood that the goal of the program was to promote safety and a sense of serenity, so she could successfully work on achieving her goals of independent living. Our session ended with her clearly requesting placement at the Safe Haven Program.

The following day, I met with Lacey and asked her if she recalled her situation just prior to entering the Respite Program and what she meant by telling me that she "can't live this way anymore?" She explained that she was sick and tired of being rejected, and having no place to stay. We reviewed how back then she really hadn't had a feasible alternative to living outside or at the shelter. She would end up staying with guys, who would use her for her SSI money, so they could buy drugs and alcohol. I said, "Even if you initially had a good time, the result was mostly the same... ending up alone, rejected and broke." Lacey was now ready to hear this gentle confrontation and spoke of her past decisions being influenced by her wanting to help others, but people would often take advantage of her. I flatly responded, "You have suffered enough, and you now have other options." Lacey appeared relieved to have another alternative to staying with others. The next day Lacey moved into the Safe Haven Program.

I continued to provide outreach-counseling and support in an effort to promote a successful transition. My work consisted of helping Lacey to continually build and utilize her toolbox of calming strategies, as well as to review and reframe program staff requests in a language that resonated in Lacey's world (bridging language), and continually promoting Lacey's self-care as a means of assuring her safety and well-being. Over the next 3 months, Safe Haven staff helped Lacey to connect into treatment at a local mental health clinic as well as manage her psychotropic medications. Lacey joined the local Clubhouse Program for adults with disabilities and this added some meaningful structure to her day. At the Clubhouse, she was able to participate in the development of a weekly newspaper utilizing a variety of artistic skills including creative writing. Lacey's sense of connection with the Clubhouse community grew and she attained greater stability. However, her improvements were not linear. After residing at the Safe Haven for approximately 8 weeks, she received her SSI check and left the program without prior notice. Lacey stayed with a past boyfriend and ended up relapsing on drugs/alcohol.

Fortunately I saw her at the park three days later. She was highly discouraged and ashamed of the poor decisions she'd made. We reviewed how it was really positive that she was self-reflective and disappointed. This indicated that she was striving to do better! The relapse counseling centered on shame reduction, which included universalizing our human frailty by reviewing that we have all made mistakes, so what is really important is to take advantage of learning opportunities. Lacey reflected on how the SSI check was a trigger toward repeating past maladaptive behaviors including trying to please men by purchasing and sharing drugs/alcohol. This conversation led to safety planning around receiving future SSI checks, as well as attending weekly Self Help Groups that address both substance abuse and codependency issues. Through successfully addressing this crisis, Lacey developed a greater sense of ownership and initiative regarding her action plan for positive change. When Lacey returned to the Safe Haven Program, she had a renewed spirit and dedication toward making healthier decisions that focused on her self-care and healing. She was now well engaged with community providers, felt comfortable at the Safe Haven Program, and began applying for future subsidized housing. My primary work was done, as Lacey embarked on her journey toward independent living with the help of dedicated Safe Haven and Clubhouse Staff, as well as Mental Health Clinicians and Self Help Groups. We made an agreement that she could call or leave a message to update me on how things were progressing. Lacey understood that our future discussions would provide short-term support, as well as redirection to appropriate services and resources.

Termination – Redefining the Relationship with Chronically Homeless Individuals

When possible, the termination process is centered on a redefinition of the current relationship by reviewing and solidifying past accomplishments, in conjunction with highlighting present providers, current supports, and the roles they can play toward promoting health and future goals. The objective is for the outreach counselor to primarily serve as a safety net that the client can readily call upon if he or she were to re-experience homelessness and/or isolation from critical supports and relationships. The termination work is centered on a redefinition rather than a complete severing of the therapeutic relationship for several reasons:

- Many people who experience chronic homelessness have had limited success in maintaining long-term relationships, and have often experienced an array of abusive relations, so it is therapeutic for them to redefine, rather than sever a healthy relationship.

- When a person has experienced the level of trauma, loss and isolation that is inherent in chronic homelessness, the therapeutic relationship that bridges the person back to housing and treatment takes on a special significance. It begins informally, and is carefully cultivated as a long-term commitment to the client's future health and success.

- People who are chronically homeless are at high risk for relapse back into homelessness. If the client were to disconnect from housing and/or treatment, the outreach counselor could very quickly provide an effective short-term intervention with the goal of restoring and/or repairing critical relationships and supports that promote stability.

The termination process with Lacey illustrates the redefinition of roles, which allows the outreach counselor to intervene in a highly directed and focused manner upon hearing that she left the Safe Haven Program. It was a very efficient process to find her and address the crisis, while utilizing the opportunity to strengthen her commitment to the Safe Haven and services. This process was facilitated because Lacey understood that the outreach counselor would remain available as a short-term support in case she was to re-experience homelessness, and the outreach counselor understood the limits of his role. It is important to pair the redefinition of roles with an active redirection of the client to appropriate providers or supports that can respond to his or her future requests or needs.

Pretreatment Principles Revisited

Lacey's narrative illustrates a trauma-informed application of pretreatment principles. The goals of promoting safety, self-care, building supports, and a greater internal sense of control are central to the work. The initial challenge is to promote short-term safety, while progressing through the stages of engagement in an effort to establish trust and a goal driven approach. The counselor used Lacey's interests and talents to facilitate common language development. These were feeding the birds, reading literature, and sketching. These themes and specific language from her hobbies were used to further the engagement process, while reinforcing her considerable strengths. Throughout the work, the outreach counselor viewed crisis as an opportunity to help Lacey develop some insight and initiative toward her goals of achieving safety and promoting self-care. The counselor's ecological considerations promoted these transitions by matching Lacey with appropriate supportive programs, and highlighted the need to enhance coping strategies. Lacey developed a toolbox to manage stress, and made some progress in dealing with environmental triggers. This provided Lacey with the internal resources and external supports needed to better manage symptoms and thereby achieve a greater sense of control, rather than being overwhelmed. The key to successful transition hinged on the availability of appropriate resources (Respite and Safe Haven programs) and the outreach worker's pairing of relationship building activities with well-timed crisis intervention. This gave Lacey the option of being placed in less stimulating environments with critical supports, while letting her know that someone really cared about her. Once Lacey felt safe and supported at the Mental Health Respite, and then again at the Safe Haven Program, she was able to utilize counseling activities that prepared her for future change including treatment and housing options. The outreach counselor understood and framed the termination process as a redefinition of roles. This enabled him to be available when Lacey relapsed, and reduced the risk of her losing well-earned gains.

The standard system of care rigidly defines program admissions and discharges, as well as the specified role of workers in relation to their programs. This could result in a loss of meaningful gains due to relapse and the inability of residential staff to do outreach beyond the program's boundaries. Also, the opportunities to re-engage individuals who may learn best during periods of crises are nullified. Relapse is a normal part of the change process and appropriately timed intervention can initiate positive change. Unfortunately, this type of powerful intervention is often short-circuited by premature program discharges back to homelessness. A chronically homeless individual is particularly vulnerable to multiple relapses. Therefore, the flexibility of the outreach worker is essential toward providing a safety net, crisis counseling, and the opportunity to re-engage clients with vital programs. Similarly, the flexibility of Safe Haven–Housing First Programs and staff to tolerate relapse by incorporating effective intervention strategies based on harm reduction principles is also critical. If we are to be successful in significantly reducing or ending long-term homelessness, then we need to utilize the full range of pretreatment strategies at our disposal. We must fully embrace the challenge of keeping people housed!

Throughout our work, it is important for outreach clinicians and Housing First staff to remain cognizant of relationship-based developmental challenges (Erikson, 1968, p. 94) of the counseling process (see Table 5 on p. 83). This is applied to the ecological phases (Germain and Gitterman, 1980) ranging from pre-engagement to termination, so the counselor can intervene accordingly. The counselor's central objective is to develop a trusting relationship that promotes safety, respects client autonomy and utilizes pretreatment strategies to foster a sense of initiative toward positive change. The power of a client-centered working alliance consoles, nurtures, and facilitates healing with survivors of trauma and homelessness. This relationship provides a safe and supportive environment, while promoting a greater sense of autonomy that empowers these emotionally fragile individuals to contemplate and prepare for relevant housing and treatment options.

Table 5. Outreach-Counseling Developmental Model

Ecological Phase	Psychosocial Challenge	Intervention
Pre-Engagement Initial Phase	Trust vs. Mistrust Issues of Safety	Observe; Identify Potential Client; Respect Personal Space; Assess Safety; Attempt Verbal & Non-Verbal Communication; Offer Essential Need Item; Listen for Client's Language; Establish Initial Communication; etc.
Engagement Initial Phase	Trust vs. Mistrust Issues of Dependency Boundary Issues	Communicate with Empathy & Authenticity; Learn Client's Language; Actively Listen by Reflecting Client's Words, Ideas, & Values; Identify & Reinforce Client Strengths; Provide Unconditional Regard; Avoid Power Struggles; Emphasize Joining the Resistance; Introduce Roles; Begin & Continue Development of Healthy Boundaries; Establish Ongoing Communication; Identify Current Life Stressors; etc.
Contracting Initial Phase	Autonomy vs. Shame Issues of Control Initiative vs. Guilt	Further Define Roles & Boundaries; Address Shame by Universalizing Human Frailty and Reviewing Client Strengths; Point Out Discrepancy & Explore Ambivalence; Negotiate Reachable Goals to Alleviate Life Stressors; Explore Client History in Relation to Goals; Determine Eligibility for Potential Resources & Services Regarding Client Interests; Further Define Shared Objectives by Utilizing Client Language; Jointly Consider Housing Options; etc.

Ecological Phase	Psychosocial Challenge	Intervention
Contract Implementation Ongoing Work Phase	Initiative vs. Guilt Issues of Stability Industry vs. Inferiority	Jointly Assess Goals, Strengths, and Obstacles; Identify and Address Fear, shame, Guilt and Anger Issues by Listening, Joining, Validating and Redirecting Focus to Achievable Tasks; Review & Reinforce Current Coping Strategies; Promote Self Care; Educate re Symptom Management; Further Develop Skills & Supports; Refer to Indicated Services; Enhance Coping Strategies; Mobilize Client Strengths; Support Transition and Adaptation to New Programs, Services and Housing; Reinforce Positive Change.
Termination Ending Phase	Relationship Identity vs. Confusion of Roles Boundary Issues Issues of Loss	Review the Work Completed Together; Emphasize Gains; Share Feelings of Loss; Connect to Past losses, while Differentiating from present loss; Reinforce & Consolidate positive Change; Review & Redefine Provider Roles, as well as Client-Worker Relationship; Review & Redirect to Established Support Systems

   * Many of the interventions listed are applicable to different phases (stages) of the outreach-counseling process, yet have particular relevance to the indicated stage.

Chapter 7 – Youth Homelessness: Freedom, Rebellion, and the Search for Camaraderie

Rousing Rebel Gal

Yellowed nicotine stained Jersey girl
Spatting out ferocious laughter as the flag unfurls
Patriotic protoplasm – She looks at with disdain
Neo-Nazi egotists have led the USA
Paranoia sprayed upon the barren wall blockades
Born again lunatics claimed to be saved!

Screw you – Boys in Blue
Leaders of the untrue

Kiss my A! – CIA
Planning another raid?

Adolescent, clandestine, independent girl
A seductive intelligence permeates her world
Well read, well-fled, Spartan tongue unfurls
A moody tattooed embittered-sweet ale
Radiating, palpitating, exonerating friend
A convalescent bond that will one day end
　　　　　—Jay S. Levy (1986) unpublished work

Dedicated to all those who have been there, survived, and have hopefully thrived.

In many ways, this poem reflects the attitudes and passions of the unaccompanied homeless youth I've met throughout our cities and towns. Many of them were hanging out on street corners or couch surfing from one semi-acquaintance to another. They ranged from 16 to 24 years old and very few, if any, had maintained a connection with their parents or former caregivers. When one ponders our impressionable years as teenagers into young adulthood and beyond, the choices that we've made and the risks that we've taken are truly astonishing. Our sense of idealism, tendency toward dualistic interpretations of events, and invulnerability coupled with youthful energy and a range of strong emotions can lead to impulsive acts or temporarily impaired judgments that can have tragic consequences. It never ceases to amaze me that so many of us have survived, let alone managed to be successful. Yet risk-taking, rebellion and experimentation are all part of testing one's limits and discovering what we will or will not become. The price of admission to adulthood is to go through these developmental crises with all the accompanied challenges such as striving for one's autonomy, while also searching for a sense of belonging. This is part and parcel of the core psychosocial challenges of adolescence and young adulthood, which include developing our self-identity, finding intimacy with others, and mastering certain educational and/or vocational skill sets in an effort to establish our independence from our parents or caregivers (Erikson, 1968; Kegan, 1982).

Most of us have experienced the often unseen advantages of being physically and mentally able, and have received needed emotional and monetary support at the right time from family and/or friends. The challenges of growing up are hard enough without piling on major trauma, neglect, addiction, mental illness, or the impact of poverty. Unfortunately, homeless youth are simultaneously confronted with developmental issues and major environmental stressors, while they are forced to contend with many, if not all of these negative factors. We therefore encounter homeless youth with a myriad of challenging presentations ranging from rebelliousness, entitlement, and fight/flight behaviors, to dependency and approach/avoidance responses, along with their many talents and compelling stories.

Youth Homelessness Policy & Data: What We Know and What We Don't Know

The US Department of Housing and Urban Development (HUD) defined unaccompanied homeless youth as being less than 25 years of age and being literally homeless by living in a homeless shelter, designated transitional homeless program, or unsheltered, which includes places not meant for human habitation such as the streets, a vehicle or an abandoned building. The Homeless Emergency Assistance and Rapid Transition to Housing (HEARTH) Act, which went into effect on January 4, 2012 expanded this definition, though HUD's yearly Point In Time count still utilizes the former definition. The newer definition (National Alliance to End Homelessness, 2012) also includes youth who are doubled up (couch surfing) and lack a permanent residence as evidenced by two moves or more over the past sixty days and who are most apt to continue to be unstably housed due to disability or multiple barriers to employment. To further complicate things, there are other federal definitions such as the Runaway and Homeless Youth Act (US Department of Health and Human Services, 2008) that states, "An individual who is not more than 21 years of age... for whom it is not possible to live in a safe environment with a relative; and has no other safe alternative living arrangement."

Meanwhile the US Department of Education's homeless student definition (2012) combines unaccompanied youth with those who live with their families in homeless shelters, or other unsheltered homeless settings. The challenge of trying to quantify, or even to begin helping homeless youth presents us with the initial difficulty of defining our terms, as well as identifying who and where they are. Many young persons without homes try to blend in with other youth, avoid adult services and resources inclusive of shelters, and may not even consider themselves to be homeless (Pope, 2009). Over the years I have met many young persons without homes who consider themselves to be free spirits or travelers, rather than acquiesce to the homeless label. However, researchers (Farrow, et al., 1992; Kenney & Shapiro, 2009) have categorized homeless youth in regard to these significant factors:

- Runaways (left home without consent of parents or caretakers)
- Throwaways (forced out of their homes by parents or

caretakers)
- Forced Removal from Home by Authorities
- Aged out of Foster Care – Approximately 25% experience homelessness
- Exited juvenile justice system
- Primarily Unsheltered/Street Youth.

Regardless of these multiple categories, conflicting definitions and our difficulties with achieving an accurate count, we know that the simultaneous impact of homelessness, poverty, and lack of a support network at a young age compromises current health and future development. Here are some sobering US statistics on health and safety that bear out this sad reality:

- Approximately 40% to 60% of homeless youth report being physically abused and 17% to 35% sexually abused (NAEH, 2006; Robertson & Toro, 1998)
- 15%-30% of youth without homes report engaging in "survival sex" (NAEH, 2009)
- 48% of youth living on the streets have either experienced a pregnancy or reported impregnating someone (Toro, Dworsky & Fowler, 2007)
- 41% report having a sexually transmitted infection, as compared to 8% of the general youth population (Kenney & Shapiro, 2009)
- 50% of homeless youth report suicidal behavior, and more than 25% have attempted suicide (Ray, 2006)
- Homeless youth are more likely to experience anxiety and mood disorders, including depression and post-traumatic stress disorder (PTSD), as well as a higher suicide rate then their housed peers (NAEH, 2006)
- Approximately 75% use illicit drugs (NAEH, 2006)
- Approximately 5,000 Youth experiencing homelessness die each year (NAEH, 2006).

Unfortunately, there are sub-populations that are even more apt to experience homelessness and its negative ramifications. Among them are young people who identify as Lesbian, Gay, Bisexual, and Transgender (LGBT). A recent survey by Durso & Gates (2012) confirms that LGBT individuals account for approximately 30- 40% of the homeless youth population. The survey found that 43% of clients served by drop-in centers and 30% of street outreach clients identified as LGBT. It also found that family rejection on the basis of sexual orientation and gender identity was the most frequently cited factor contributing to LGBT homelessness. In addition, LGBT youth without homes are even more likely to experience mental health issues and attempt suicide compared to their heterosexual peers (Durso & Gates, 2012; NAEH, 2008). When we are working with LGBT youth, or homeless youth in general, our major goals include assuring safety, promoting acceptance, and facilitating a sense of belonging. These statistics are even more alarming when we consider the societal costs (moral, fiscal, and quality of life considerations) of young people being severely hurt and potentially struggling for many years to come.

Helping Homeless Youth

It is evident that most homeless youth have experienced signifi-cant trauma, so a trauma informed approach is crucial to our success with engagement, goal setting, and addressing treatment issues. This is complicated by the developmental challenges that youth face, which often manifest as a push for autonomy and independence regardless of its costs and without a mature under-standing of what this actually entails, or how it ultimately affects themselves and/or others. It is important to note that there are programs throughout the country, though not nearly enough, that serve homeless youth. In particular, street outreach teams and drop-in centers with access to a comprehensive set of resources and services inclusive of supportive and independent housing have been successful. Drop-in centers, club-houses, educational/vocational programs are able to nurture a culture that accepts folks "where they are at" and form a sense of community, empowerment and belonging matched by a reasonable set of limits or rules. They provide a safe and respectful environment where youth can flourish (Schneir et al., 2007). Encouraging a group process among program participants to celebrate achievements, as well as giving voice to what basic rules are needed, the reasons why, and how to enforce them are helpful toward fostering a sense of control and community connection (Schneir et al., 2007, Levy, 2010).

Working with people's strengths, artistic talents and interests is a highly effective manner of promoting engagement, while respecting the diversity of program participants. This may include the use of creative expression techniques to help youth depict their reality and find perspective through an artistic language that includes listening to, composing and discussing poetry and/or music (i.e. folk, rap, hip-hop, rock, etc.), as well as creative writing, journaling, sketching and/or painting, etc. Since many of the homeless youth that we meet are quite tech savvy, resource centers and programs of all types could benefit their participants by developing interactive software to provide targeted information and eligibility criteria to meet individualized needs such as enrolling in GED classes or college courses, as well as accessing recommended housing and educational/vocational websites, blogs, and chat rooms. This will provide some participants with the freedom to find these resources unobtrusively, or even develop a support network through the click of a mouse or touch technology.

Other programs that have contributed to the success of young people including homeless youth are vocational/education programs with a residential component such as: Job Corps (jobcorps.gov), which is a nationwide Federal program that focuses on attaining a GED, building job skills, and career development from the ages of 16 years old to 24 years old. Homelessness is not a disqualifying criterion. Also, working farms with a housing component and support staff can foster a sense of community, and can help working age youth develop new marketable skills. One such farm that serves homeless young adults and others with past legal issues is Dismas House Farm (www.dismashouse.org). Another type of educational/ vocational program is Boston University's Center for Psychiatric Rehabilitation (http://cpr.bu.edu/about). It is an innovative program that provides college type rehabilitative classes and vocational counseling that can be paired with dorms for individuals with major mental health concerns. Targeted services and resources via youth shelters, transitional residences, drop in centers, vocational programs, and outreach teams, among others, continue to have a positive impact. However, additional funding sources are needed to make programs like these plentiful, affordable, and accessible to homeless youth.

A psychiatric rehabilitative approach (Anthony, Cohen & Farkas, 1990) works well with the idealism, high energy, and demands of youth because it starts from peoples' goals and desires and then proceeds to jointly define barriers to reaching those objectives. Starting with their goals helps youth to get focused on how to develop the necessary skills, supports, and environmental modifications necessary for success. Even an initial unrealistic goal could still lead to useful skill development, or through the process of jointly assessing barriers to its achievement, a person may choose to modify a goal into something that is more reachable. I also recommend utilizing Solution Focus Brief Therapy (SFBT) oriented questions to facilitate the goal making process or contracting stage (Walter & Peller, 1992; Levy, 1998) as follows: "What changes would you like to see in your life? If you had three wishes to change your current situation, what would you wish for? If a miracle were to happen today, what would be different?" A solution-focused approach recommends following up these questions by exploring how current behaviors support or obstruct identified goals. Both a Psychiatric Rehabilitation Model and SFBT are proven approaches to facilitate the contracting and contract implementation stages of outreach and engagement.

Pretreatment Applications

For many years we have known that a major key to success is to develop a client centered relationship (Rogers, 1957; Levy, 1998; Wampold, 2001). Based on this knowledge, I introduced a developmental model of outreach and engagement (Levy, 1998; Levy, 2000) to promote the pretreatment principle of relationship formation, which is the foundation of outreach work. This approach has been successfully integrated with the delivery of Homeless Outreach services in Boston, Worcester, Western Massachusetts, and many other areas throughout the country. In fact, three recent publications on youth homelessness (Aviles & Helfrich, 2006; Bender, et al., 2007; McManus and Thompson, 2008) reviewed its merits of serving hard to engage populations such as homeless youth. Further, McManus and Thompson (2008) discuss how the Outreach Counseling-Developmental Model (see Table 5 on p. 83) and its intervention strategies based on Erickson's (1968) psychosocial developmental stages correspond with the tasks of adolescence and is an effective approach with homeless youth who have experienced significant trauma.

As highlighted throughout Lacey's narrative (Chapter 6), pretreatment is a trauma-informed practice. Its universal guiding principles of clinical care can help inform youth service delivery in many ways. This includes outreach teams, shelter and residential staff, Housing First counselors and drop-in center case managers. Patience is needed when serving homeless youth. Inevitably, part of the change and learning process will be accompanied by frequent backsliding. The success of these programs and services often hinges upon the skills of the staff to actively engage, promote trust and respect the autonomy of homeless youth, while artfully facilitating appropriate boundaries, as well as developing a common language in an effort to define goals, and thereby access needed resources/ services. Other central challenges consist of supporting transitions to housing and treatment, as well as promoting the safety and well-being of clients. In particular, it is difficult but crucial to balance harm reduction approaches that uphold a person's sense of autonomy with crisis intervention strategies that can be more directive. This helps to assure a young person's safety. With this in mind, the narratives throughout this book are provided as a resource to explore the intricacies of applying pretreatment principles to real life situations. The next chapter is a narrative of my work with a 19 year old self-identified gay, white male named Anthony. I hope that his story will help us to better understand some of the significant challenges and best practices for assisting young people without homes, as well as further demonstrate how a pretreatment approach can be a helpful guide.

Chapter 8 – Anthony's Narrative: Navigating Tumultuous Waters

> "I love to cook! My dream is to own a cafe... just like this one!"
>
> – Anthony

The Power of Acceptance

I remember back in the 1980s, when we suddenly saw many young people coming into NYC's shelters or ending up on the streets, reporting that their families kicked them out because they were gay. This was at the height of HIV/AIDS hysteria. At this period in time, the media reported on renowned people making ludicrous statements that declared the AIDS epidemic as a punishment from God for choosing a gay lifestyle. I could not bear to see people with life threatening illnesses being treated with such disrespect and scorn. It was unbearable to meet young men who were depressed and confused by the rejection of their own family, while trying to deal with what was then considered a terminal illness. To make things worse, the shelters were not safe places for someone who was gay, let alone for someone who was prone to infection. People living in such close quarters were exposed to a whole host of infectious agents, while also being harassed, abused, and victimized. During that period, I did my best to help. The task was enormous considering all of the obstacles, societal pressures, medical complications, and the lack of safe alternative environments. This was a personal turning point for me. I realized more than ever the power of acceptance, which was the one thing that I could surely deliver, and it was cherished by everyone I encountered. If we were really going to help those most in need, then everything must start with acceptance. It is a relationship that is built on trust and respect for "where people are at," which makes everything else possible.

Pre-engagement & Engagement

Many years later on a hot summer day, I met Anthony at a community meal program in Western Massachusetts. He was a slender, well dressed, 19-year-old white male sitting alone with his legs crossed and carefully attending to his soup and sandwich. Right next to him sat a strategically placed, overfilled backpack. At first I was hesitant to approach, believing that he was not homeless, but I was also struck by his isolation and his backpack that was bursting at the seams. Upon my approach, he greeted me with a half-smile, while gazing down at his food. We spoke for a short while and he revealed with a slightly anxious voice that approximately one year ago, shortly after graduating from high school, he had a major conflict with his mother and was forced to leave his home. When I asked him how he got by without much income or a place to live, he explained that he received welfare benefits, even though he would prefer to work. Where he resided was much more complicated. At first he stayed in a local motel, but after two weeks he'd depleted all of his savings. He then enrolled in Job Corps, a residential youth vocational training program, but didn't make it past the orientation. After couch surfing for a few months, Anthony stayed a couple of months with a relative, but was asked to leave after they had a heated argument. I purposely steered our initial conversation away from the content of his interpersonal difficulties and instead explained that I was a Homeless Outreach worker who may be able to help him find a safe place to stay. At that point, Anthony made direct eye contact and in a stern voice said, "One thing you should know is that I am gay, and if you can't deal with that, then I don't need your help!" Surprised, but with well-learned lessons from my past, I responded: "I'm here to help you and I promise to respect who you are, while doing my best to help."

Fortunately, much had changed since the 1980s, though certain stereotypes and prejudices remained. I knew of a small shelter whose supervisor was openly gay. I described the shelter, which fit the description of a rundown quaint house, and the openness of the staff to serve people from all walks of life. Furthermore, the shelter only served up to 16 men and women at a time, which made the environment reasonably quiet and private in comparison to larger shelters. Anthony immediately showed an interest and I was able to facilitate placement that same evening. However, I left our meeting concerned about whether or not Anthony would be successful at following the rules of the shelter, as well as his ability to get along with others.

Later that week I discovered that both of these concerns were quite valid. As it turned out, Anthony had a long trauma history consisting of numerous beatings by his step dad, and was further wounded by his mother's inability to embrace his gay identity. Worse than that, she was directly hostile to his sexual orientation and this led to his departure from his childhood home into the uncertain world of young adulthood. This history of trauma in conjunction with the developmental stage of young adulthood often leads to questioning and rejecting authority, as well as general difficulties with trusting one's peers. An additional layer that further complicates matters is that someone who is gay will encounter very real biases and abuses that could put their health and safety at risk, while posing a direct challenge to their search for intimacy and developing a sense of belonging. Understandably, Anthony was very sensitive to any perceived mistreatment from others, and this set in motion a dynamic that invariably led to interpersonal conflict. Often, but not always, Anthony responded in a disproportionate manner to someone being disrespectful or lacking sensitivity to his plight. Any sense of disrespect, including when staff told him to do a household chore, rather than a polite inquiry, caused Anthony to go into a rage. This consisted of belligerent language followed by him storming off to his shelter bed or leaving the shelter, while shouting expletives. Unfortunately, a couple of the shelter guests fed into these negative behaviors by taunting him with derogatory and abusive slogans that belittled him for being gay, such as "Once again, the little fagot is having a hissy fit." I share this not to be crude, but to make readers aware of the cruelty that Anthony was forced to endure.

My work was twofold. First, it was to remain connected with Anthony, regardless of his outbursts toward others, and help him to appreciate that his exceedingly strong reactions had and would continue to undermine his future prospects. Second, I needed to consult with staff on how best to respond to Anthony's acting-out behaviors, while also advising them to set strong limits on hate speech by other shelter guests. Fortunately, the shelter supervisor was very empathic to Anthony's plight and responsive to my feedback. This resulted in the shelter manager making an immediate declaration of a zero tolerance policy for hate speech in regard to race, religion, creed, color, sex, age, gender identity, and sexual orientation. This was clearly posted on the wall, with an understanding that violation of this policy would mean an immediate warning and possible dismissal from the shelter. Looking back on it now, this was a very positive outcome that was directly derived from social conflict rising to a point of crisis. My goal was to re-engage with Anthony and give him some assurance around the new shelter policy, as well as offer needed support, guidance, and counsel.

Solution Focused Work: Crisis Intervention and Contracting

Later that same day, I caught up with Anthony and he was less communicative and appeared hesitant to engage. Sensing this difficulty, and instead of immediately focusing on the turmoil that had just transpired, I invited Anthony to come join me for a cold beverage at a local cafe. After all, it was ninety degrees outside and Anthony needed a break from the shelter environment. Once we were seated and calmly sipping our ice teas, I asked, "What would you like to see happen in your life? I mean... If you had the power to change or do anything, what would it be?" As it turned out, the timing was right and Anthony was ready to talk about his aspirations. He said, "I just want to get away from all the craziness. You know what calms me the most?" As I began to shake my head; Anthony blurted out, "I love to cook! My dream is to own a cafe... just like this one! I could plan the menu and prepare the cuisine, or even manage it. People would come from everywhere just to enjoy my specialties."

At first, I was speechless; this was what we refer to in narrative circles as a "sparkling moment" or a chance to "work with the exception." In other words, Anthony's statement focused on his strengths and dreams, rather than being centered on his problems and deficits. I responded, "That's a wonderful vision! Maybe we can figure out some reachable goals that will get you closer to making that a reality. I recently heard about a job training program that teaches food preparation and cooking skills. I don't remember all the details, but I could look into it for you. If you're willing to work with me, I think I could help." Anthony agreed and we contracted to focus our energies toward making his dream an eventual reality.

In fact, I knew of a new culinary arts training program geared toward serving homeless individuals with mental illnesses. It partnered with a local MH Clubhouse vocational program, which provided job coaches and support workers for members who were interested in being certified in food safety and helped them to work in the culinary arts field. This allowed students to train in food preparation, so they could assist area chefs at hotel restaurants, while also providing a subsidized housing placement with ongoing support services. However, I decided to temporarily hold off on sharing this particular resource because I needed to further explain things so Anthony could better understand the role of Clubhouses and not be turned off or feel stigmatized by the label of mental illness. More to the point, I needed to first address some of the significant interpersonal issues that could put this plan at risk. I said to Anthony, "There is one thing that gets me worried... I really want to see you succeed, yet I am concerned about all the recent conflicts at the shelter and I get the sense that it has been a real struggle to deal with others... Can you tell me how you look at things?"

At that moment, Anthony began to share his story of abuse, neglect and rejection due to his sexual orientation. He understood his rage as righteous anger for being ignored and mistreated. I initially responded by informing Anthony of the recent changes at the shelter to protect him and others from hateful speech. I told him that I certainly respected his right to identify himself as a gay male and so did the supervisor of the shelter, which was one of the main reasons why they instituted the new policy. Those who made hateful remarks had been warned and we wanted to assure his safety and well-being. Anthony was taken aback by all of this and was able to see, at least for the moment, that people really did care. He said, while looking down and close to tears, "I can't believe that they would do that for me. I'm really touched."

At that point we were well engaged, and I could tell that my words had meaning in Anthony's world. A conversational ease was established and I took advantage of this by once again sharing my concerns around the degree that Anthony acted out his anger. I said, "I'm glad you can see that people are making efforts to improve things, but that also puts the onus on you to try and manage how you treat others. Do you know what I mean?" Anthony once again described all the things that got him angry. I gently interrupted and said, "I understand why you get angry and you have every right to your anger, I'm just concerned about the way it gets expressed. It sometimes comes across as just too much... What I mean is that not every disagreeable situation warrants the same type of response."

Anthony thought about this for a moment and responded with insight, while also letting me know that he would not tolerate much more on this topic, "If you'd been through what I have been through you'd respond the same way!" To help bring things to a close and to set up future work I said, "You are right about that. I'd respond the same way. It is not your fault that you have been through so much pain. I'd like to help you to manage some of the pain and anger, so you can be more successful in your interactions with others, whether it be at the shelter, or in the future when you are managing your own café." Anthony nodded as the intensity of our ninety minute conversation began to wane. We left off with a plan to meet again in a couple of days so I could share more information on vocational programs, as well as follow up on developing skills and supports for managing anger and rage. This was a major step in reconstructing Anthony's narrative with concern for interpersonal relations and directly relating it to his future aspirations. By doing this, it set the stage for our work on how to better get along with others and stay safe, while also developing the critical skills of conflict resolution and regulating emotions, which were needed for Anthony to be successful at work and in life.

As I left our meeting and made my way back to the shelter, I reflected on a few things. I believed that beginning our conversation with an offer to go get a cold drink and being solution focused, rather than immediately focusing on the recent conflict at the shelter, was crucial toward successfully engaging Anthony in a lengthy and productive conversation. This consisted of helping him to be goal centered, so we could begin planning the steps for positive change. Anthony could then make an effort to reorganize his behaviors around attaining these goals. In short, we needed to find a meaningful purpose to help motivate behavioral change, and his desire to manage a café and/or become a chef seemed to fit the bill. This also brought to the forefront the complex issue of job readiness versus the need to apply for or remain on welfare or disability benefits. While it is important to work with someone's dreams, it can be difficult to judge a young person's current or potential level of vocational functioning. When I served young adults, who had limited work histories and the promise of a long future, it was particularly important to try a myriad of educational/ vocational and supportive employment options. Fortunately, there were vocational training programs geared toward helping folks with disabilities and were quite savvy on how to achieve an individualized plan that balances the need for benefits with work opportunities. This seemed to be the right path for Anthony since he was already on welfare benefits, yet had expressed interest in attaining work. We now had the option of learning about the level of his vocational functioning as we went, while still applying for social security benefits just in case his plan to work was unrealistic. In a very real way, Anthony had embarked upon an experiment to test his vocational abilities.

Two days later I dropped by the shelter and Anthony appeared highly distraught. He was very angry and it was evident by both his demeanor and the way he was slamming things onto the kitchen counter while he prepared a snack. I calmly walked into the kitchen and asked if anything was wrong. He then went into a rant on how nobody cared about him and how tired he was of this godforsaken shelter. I invited him to speak in private and he agreed to meet in an office that was situated right off the main dining area.

Supporting Transitions: Managing Crisis and Contract Implementation

Once we were seated, I asked Anthony if anything was bothering him. He replied, "Nobody wants to talk with me. Now that they got these new rules all I get is the silent treatment and I'm not going to stand for it!" I responded, "One of the hardest things is to find acceptance. You are not alone in wanting to be respected, but you can't control what others do. Let's focus on what you can actually do, while being here. Do you know what I mean?" He responded meekly, with a diverted gaze, "You don't know what I'm going through. Last night I felt so down, I just started cutting myself." Anthony then proceeded to roll up his sleeves and revealed some well-aged cuts and scratches on one arm, paired with fresher wounds on his other arm. None of the cuts looked particularly deep, nor was there any current bleeding, but I was nevertheless alarmed. After a deep breath, I said, "Anthony, when I see all those cuts I get worried about your safety. Clearly, this is not the first time you've done this. Have you ever gotten any help for this issue?" Anthony shared his history of cutting along with his history of mental health counseling and psychiatry. This included an involuntary inpatient stay when he was 16 years old. As difficult as this session was, psychiatry and mental health considerations were now on the table and our common language had now broadened from gay identity issues, past trauma, and vocational pursuits to discussing his mood fluctuations, unstable mental states, and past mental health treatment approaches. After some further discussion, I remarked: "It sounds like your mood fluctuates a great deal from day-to-day, or maybe even within the same day. I say that because just two days ago we had drawn up a plan around your dream of working and owning a cafe, and now you are letting me know how depressed and empty you can feel... Like there is absolutely no one who cares. Is that a fair statement?" Anthony nodded and once again went on to explain how often he was mistreated and how angry this made him. After doing my best to reflect back his words and his strong feelings of being hurt and enraged, I said, "There is definitely a relationship between the level of pain you've experienced throughout your life and the degree of outrage and anger you've expressed. No one can blame you for those feelings, but I still get concerned over how this impacts your ability to interact with others. We need to create a space where you can feel a sense of purpose and belonging, as opposed to spending most of your energy on perpetual conflicts. Does that make sense?" This once again brought the issue back to the here and now, as well as put the ball in his court for action, rather than just feeling stuck and overwhelmed with feelings of despair or rage. Anthony agreed that he would like to see that happen, but was perplexed over what to do or how to begin.

In response to this dilemma and within the context of Anthony's unfolding narrative, we explored meaningful options. I asked, "When you were really upset, where did I find you?" Anthony replied, "I was in the kitchen preparing a snack." I exclaimed, "Exactly! You already know what helps you through some of these feelings... Maybe we could set something up via the shelter supervisor that would allow you to prepare the nightly snack for shelter guests... Not necessarily every night, but I'm sure that they could use a few more volunteers!" For the first time during our meeting, Anthony smiled and not only was in agreement, but boasted, "If I'm given a chance, I could definitely improve the snack menu!" Buoyed by Anthony's openness to food preparation and realizing that we had already discussed the concept of mental health via his psychiatric history, I added, "The culinary arts program we spoke about at our last meeting is available via the local Clubhouse where they help people with histories of mental health concerns focus on recovery and employment. If you are interested, we could set up a tour, so we could learn more about it." Feeling supported and heard, Anthony agreed to the tour and seemed once again excited about his future prospects. Our meeting ended with a safety assessment and Anthony assured me that he felt much better and in control. He shared, "I wasn't trying to kill myself, but I sometimes feel so numb that I don't know what to do." This led to our conversation on developing formalized stress and anger management options derived from what had worked for him in the past. In response, we wrote a list of coping strategies down on an index card that he could keep safely in his wallet for future use to avert emergencies. These coping strategies included taking a long shower to promote relaxation, going on short walks to take a break from things, and playing certain songs to help inspire him, as well as doing a fun activity such as cooking. At the very bottom of the card I included and highlighted the number to the local mental health crisis team, which was available 24/7 for assessment, counsel and consultation. We left off with a plan to meet the next day, so we could once again review his coping strategies and how to utilize the crisis team, as well as follow up on scheduling the Clubhouse tour and snack preparation via the shelter. It was now evident to me that my work with Anthony during this phase remained quite intensive. My hope was to help Anthony build a support network, so he could practice coping strategies, as well as turn to others when he felt mistreated, rejected, and alone.

The following day I attended a meeting with shelter staff and they were quite thankful for my work with Anthony. I explained to the staff some of the interpersonal difficulties Anthony had experienced including his struggles for acceptance by others as a young gay man. I recommended that they assign a caseworker who could be supportive around these issues, as well as connect him with a Healthcare for the Homeless nurse who could respond to his medical needs, as well as review HIV/AIDS risk and safe sex practices. Anthony could certainly benefit by having others who he could check-in with on a daily basis. Earl was assigned as his shelter case manager and later that day the three of us met to discuss the topic of shelter snack preparation. This was a perfect way to acquaint Anthony with Earl, as well as to directly connect them with Anthony's goal of cooking for others. Anthony and I also reviewed his newly formulated coping strategies and added Earl and me as supportive contacts he could turn to for assistance. We wrote the expanded list of coping strategies down on an index card and Anthony placed the card in his wallet with the understanding that whenever it was needed, he could quickly access it for guidance. That night, Anthony baked brownies for shelter snack and it was a big hit. From that day forward, Anthony prepared shelter snack three times per week and, with Earl's assistance, he even went shopping for groceries. A couple of days later he had his first appointment with Healthcare for the Homeless, and it went very well.

The next week, I referred Anthony to the local MH Clubhouse, and within one month's time he began volunteering in the kitchen to prepare a daily free lunch for fellow Clubhouse members. Clubhouses or Social Clubs follow psychosocial rehabilitation principles, as opposed to a medical model of diagnosis, illness and treatment of symptoms. The Clubhouses focus on self-help, friendship, recreational activities, housing, and establishing meaningful and gainful employment among other things. When working with youth, it is extremely helpful to find an environment where they can find a sense of acceptance and community. Other resources I have utilized when available include: Youth Drop-In Centers, Recovery Learning Centers, and Vocational/Educational training facilities. I felt fortunate to secure Anthony a Clubhouse placement that was within walking distance of the shelter.

After six weeks of working with Anthony, it was evident that he had made great strides. He had successfully shared his culinary skills with both shelter guests and Clubhouse members, while meeting with Earl and me on a regular basis for case management and outreach counseling services. However, Anthony remained reticent toward getting Mental Health treatment and was growing increasingly impatient with waiting for an opening in the culinary arts training program.

Our newfound success had hit a snag. I received a phone call from a Clubhouse advocate notifying me that Anthony had just stormed off the premises. He reportedly had a major run-in with another Clubhouse member and got angry with the staff when they did not immediately take his side. I went over to the shelter and Earl (Shelter Case Manager) quickly got my attention and reported that Anthony announced that he was leaving and was currently at his bunk packing up his stuff. I approached Anthony and asked, "What's going on?" Anthony responded in an angry and dejected tone, "I am getting out of here! People just want to take advantage of me and I'm not going to put up with it." I responded, "Anthony, I am confused... What just happened? Why are you leaving?" He went on to say that one of the Clubhouse members was bossing him around the kitchen and that everyone was using him to get free meals. He then stated, "Look... I've been cooking and helping out for weeks and still I haven't been offered a space in the culinary arts program. This is a bunch of bull!" I then noticed that there was some blood slowly dripping down his right arm and I knew that I needed to act fast, so I could assess his safety and hopefully help him to reconsider his current plan. I said, "I know that when you wait for something it can feel like it's never going to happen and it also sounds like that whatever went on at the Clubhouse really hurts. Right now, you're upset and your arm is bleeding. Let's take a breather and tend to your wounds." Anthony looked down and fell silent. After about 30 seconds, which seemed like an eternity, I said, "Come on Anthony; let's get you some water and bandages, so we can chat." Anthony agreed and we made our way to the bathroom to wash off his self- inflicted wounds. Thankfully, these appeared to be just surface scratches and the bleeding had stopped.

Upon our return from the bathroom, I established direct eye contact and said, "Anthony, I'm here for the long haul. Please don't forget that when things get hard, we can talk." We then spent the next thirty minutes discussing his expectations and the merits of the vocational-food preparation program. I assured him that the culinary arts program and the attached subsidized housing were real, but that it would still take about 3-4 weeks before they'd have another opening. In the meantime, I offered to set up an orientation meeting with the program case manager, who worked at the Clubhouse. He then said in a rapid voice with notable anxiety, "I think I blew it... I don't even know if they'll let me back there. I was so enraged that I told off the staff." I responded in a calm and reassuring manner, while using his expressed concern as leverage, "I think that if you went to the local MH Clinic to work on things with a therapist, that would definitely help us to advocate for your return to the Clubhouse." Thankfully, Anthony was on board with that idea. We then proceeded to talk about his inner struggle and how that could sap motivation and become a barrier to success. I often frame this as a conflict between the different parts of our-selves.

I explained this to Anthony in the following way, "I can clearly see that you are talented, intelligent and that you are really striving to do better, while at the same time another part of you is understandably hurt, angry and impatient. After all, you've been wounded by all the abuse you've been through. Perhaps therapy will help you to better understand these different aspects of who you are and align yourself more fully with your goals." He commented, while slowly shaking his head, "I am so tired of fighting myself and others. Maybe seeing a therapist will help... I don't know. I certainly appreciate how much you've been there for me." I again responded, "Thank you Anthony... That means a great deal to me. I'll continue to be there for you, but I also want you to have a safe place where you can explore the challenges of being a gay male in a society that is not very tolerant. Hopefully, you and your therapist can establish the type of relationship where you can comfortably talk about these types of things." Our session ended with a review of the list of coping strategies, which he kept securely in his wallet. Ironically, when he was pulling the index card from his wallet it exposed a razor blade that was hidden underneath. Anthony then took out the razor blade, held it up in plain sight, and announced, "I don't need this anymore!"

Contract Implementation, Termination, and Redefining the Relationship

As it turned out, Anthony began attending therapy sessions and even agreed to a medication assessment by a psychiatrist, while continuing to receive medical services via Healthcare for the Homeless. His psychiatrist prescribed him Trazodone, a psycho-tropic medication that can help improve sleep, as well as reduce symptoms of anxiety and depression. Anthony agreed to give it a try. In turn, the Clubhouse accepted him back, and within four weeks' time he began attending classes to earn a culinary arts training certificate and possible job placement. This also led to him being assigned a case manager via the Next Step program. The Next Step program runs in conjunction with the Clubhouse and provides support staff in regard to job training, placement, and coaching services, as well as housing search, placement, and ongoing residential support services. Once Anthony was enrolled in the Next Step program, he was awarded a housing voucher (HUD funded) that could be accepted by a landlord to subsidize his new apartment at thirty percent of his income.

None of this came easily. There were several more incidents along the way that mirrored what has already been shared. Regardless of the particular underpinnings and specifics of the crisis or conflict at hand, it was critical for me, as an outreach counselor, to remain available and patient. At times it was akin to navigating and steering through rough seas. It took a steady hand! In this case, I maintained a consistent and accepting presence with an eye toward staying on course for goal attainment. Anthony continued to struggle with managing interpersonal issues and I spoke to the part of him that desperately wanted a better life, while remaining optimistic and solution focused. I used the cognitive reminder of "Keep your eye on the ball!" I emphatically said to Anthony, "Let's not get lost in the details or minor conflicts; instead we need to concentrate on you and what is important for your future." We also did a weekly review of coping strategies, before I redirected him back to others who had become an increasingly vital part of his support network. Since our first meeting, Anthony's support system had grown considerably. It now included Clubhouse members/staff, and a Next Step case manager, as well as his therapist, psychiatrist, shelter case manager (Earl), and me. Anthony consistently attended his vocational training program where he had positive interactions with both the instructor and his classmates. He did well in class and was very proud of his newfound skills and knowledge of safe food preparation. Most impressively, since the day that Anthony gave me his razor blade, there were no further incidents of cutting. It seemed like he had successfully funneled (sublimated) much of his anger away from himself and toward proving that others were wrong about him. He now wanted to succeed, in order to get back at all the people who had sold him short and did him wrong. His anger was now fueling positive change! This made me wonder what would happen if Anthony were to suddenly believe that he failed to reach his goals. Could this result in his anger being once again turned inward and him becoming a heightened suicide risk, or even an expression of outward aggression toward others? Though I remained unconvinced that this put Anthony at greater risk, I was still comforted to know that he could now attain help from an array of care providers including the Clubhouse community.

After being at the shelter for approximately four months, Anthony was offered subsidized housing with Next Step support services. His move-in date was scheduled to occur within two weeks and we were excited to celebrate his success. Surprisingly, Anthony walked into the common area and appeared to be upset. I invited him to sit down so we could talk, and Anthony shared the following with notable anger: "People can't wait to see me go. Nobody wants me to stay here!" I responded, "Anthony, we're proud of what you have accomplished and we want to celebrate it! I want you to know that we'll miss you. I worked closely with you and I am proud that you are ready to take the next step." After a momentary pause Anthony declared, "I want you and everyone else to know that I don't need or want a celebration!" He then abruptly left the room. Upon his leaving, I was once again reminded of the difficulties many of our clients faced. Anthony and I had forged a significant helping relationship at a very vulnerable time in his life. My expectation for him to be happy about getting housed did not factor in the depth of our relationship and his feelings around loss and rejection. The truth was that over the past month, Anthony could sense my pulling away as others became more central to achieving his future plans. This was purposeful, but we had not spent enough time discussing this gradual, yet steady change in our relationship. As mentioned during chapter six (Lacey's Narrative), redefining the relationship is one of the central tasks of termination and this is particularly important with impressionable youth who lack parental guidance. In that moment, immediately following my reflection on the difficulties of termination, I was cognizant of the challenges that lay directly ahead.

During the next week, Anthony kept his interactions with Earl and me purposely brief. In response, we decided to try and break the ice with a peace offering that would show how much we valued him and his accomplishments. The next day, after Anthony left the shelter to attend class, Earl and I decorated the common area with streamers and we prepared a cake to congratulate him on his achievements. We were also able to get several shelter guests to participate in warmly welcoming him back from school. When Anthony first arrived, he was absolutely shocked! His eyes began to well up with tears, as we all gave him a long round of applause. I then briefly addressed the group, "Anthony, you have shown us a fine example of how to succeed regardless of difficult circumstances. Not only have you continued to do well at school, but in a few days you'll be moving to your own subsidized apartment. Congratulations from all of us!" This was followed by Anthony gladly cutting the cake and he was once again feeling connected. All in all, this was a much healthier outcome for him than holding on to the vestiges of pain, anger, and rejection.

After the celebration, Anthony and I sat down to meet. We spent the time reviewing his many transitions and successes from first entering the shelter to becoming a Clubhouse member, as well as enrolling in the Next Step Program and participating in the culinary arts training program. We also reviewed the array of ongoing supports and what role each person served from his therapist and psychiatrist to his Next Step case manager. I also reminded him of the razor he'd given me in exchange for his index card of coping strategies. We both knew that it was the nature of our relationship and not the card in and of itself that empowered Anthony to take such a bold step. Yet, within the context of termination, the index card served the additional purpose of being a meaningful transitional object that represented both our work and Anthony's hard-earned gains. Together, we recognized that Anthony had shown great courage to walk down the path toward uncertain change. It was Anthony who'd first agreed to work with me despite his history of abuse. He also chose to walk through the door of the Clubhouse and begin attending food preparation classes, when turning away could have avoided the dual risk of rejection and failure. In short, it was Anthony who took all of the major risks. My role was to provide consistent support and guidance, until Anthony could develop the skills and the needed supports to succeed. While this may have been our last formal session, it certainly wasn't our last meeting. Anthony understood that I'd remain available in case of a crisis that could put his housing at risk, though I would direct him back to ongoing services and available resources for further help. He also knew that I wanted to attend his graduation from culinary arts school and he promised to invite me to the Clubhouse sponsored ceremony. We then agreed to stay in touch and, with that, solidified the redefinition of our relationship.

Shortly thereafter, Anthony moved into his new apartment and continued to get support services through the Clubhouse and Next Step. He successfully graduated from the culinary arts training program and began some food prep work at a local hotel restaurant. A few months later he dropped by to say hello. Near the end of our brief visit, Anthony turned to me and said, "I'll never forget all that you've done for me. I did my best to leave on a sour note and you wouldn't have it. I want to thank you for believing in me." I smiled and said, "Anthony, I'll never stop believing in you!" He then shook my hand and headed for the exit. As I made my way back to the meal program where Anthony and I'd first met, I thought to myself that it's unusual in my line of work to get direct thanks, but this one was well worth the wait.

Chapter 9 – Housing First: From Concept to Working Models

Every house where love abides
And friendship is a guest
Is surely home, and home sweet home
For there the heart can rest.

–from "A Home Song"
by Henry van Dyke, (1909)

Housing First: Why, What, and How?

We inherently understand the importance of having a home, and yet throughout the years there were many people without homes who fell between the cracks and never received the affordable housing and support services they so desperately needed. The old continuum of care model (prior to the availability of Housing First options) was based on the notion of offering treatment first and graduating people from one program to another as a path to independent housing. Though well intentioned, it was arguably in part to blame for a burgeoning chronically homeless population. Ongoing issues with the continuum of care model ranged from restrictive eligibility criteria that excluded people from accessing needed housing with support services (Levy, 2010) to the assumption that those who graduated through the continuum could be successfully housed without ongoing support services (Tsemberis 1999, p. 227). Other salient issues were that most continuums of care housing programs showed little relapse tolerance and viewed treatment as prerequisite to enter. Further, refusal of treatment after placement in a residential program was a violation that warranted expulsion from both the housing and the attached services. This meant that the residential staff and counselors who knew the client best were no longer available to help. The result was that many people experiencing episodic and long-term homelessness continued to be at increased risk for an array of medical issues, premature death, and escalating medical costs due to frequent emergency room usage and inpatient stays. In response to the growing individual and societal costs of chronic homelessness, Housing First programs were developed and researched as either an alternative to the continuum of care approach or as an addition to continuum of care housing options that better serve the full range of homeless subgroups. Integrating a Housing First and harm reduction philosophy with traditional continuum of care options is a significant undertaking, but well worth the effort to enable the best fit (not exact match) between housing, support services, and individual need.

The Pathways to Housing program, and HUD funded Safe Haven programs, were key ingredients of the Housing First movement during the 1990s. Since then, many so-called Housing First programs and approaches have been propagated throughout the country, and this has caused some confusion as to the meaning of the term. As stated earlier (see Chapter 3), Housing First does not require a person to accept or participate in mental health, addiction or medical treatment, nor does it demand that they achieve sobriety prior to being housed. The basic premise was to help the most vulnerable among the homeless as quickly as possible. This meant reaching out, rapidly housing and providing support services to people with significant disabilities who were at high risk of injury, exacerbation of chronic conditions, acute illnesses, or death. The hope has always been that the housing support service would help folks to consider and eventually choose needed community resources, services and treatment, as opposed to it being mandated as a prior condition to getting housed. This short-circuits the old continuum of care model by directly providing permanent housing with support services to those in dire need, rather than a system that measures progress by graduating people from one program to another. The fundamentals of Housing First are a timely offer of affordable housing matched with outreach services to support transition and housing stabilization, as well as respecting client choice in regard to participation in treatment. In some cases, the concept of Housing First has been expanded to include providing affordable housing as quickly as possible without concern for the client's vulnerability, chronic homeless status, or need for support services. However, my work experience, the case narratives and research in this book have repeatedly shown that support services are an essential ingredient for helping chronically homeless and/or highly vulnerable individuals.

Working Models: Pathways to Housing, REACH, and Safe Havens

The genesis of Housing First models and formal research can be traced back to the Pathways to Housing program, which was started during 1992 by Dr. Tsemberis. Its design is based on five basic principles and values:

1. Rapid access to permanent and affordable housing and rapidly re-house, rather than long stretches of homelessness.

2. Uphold consumer choice and respect the consumer's decision in regard to treatment – based on psychosocial rehabilitation principles, it is best to proceed with treatment when the client actively chooses that path.

3. Separation of housing from services: If a client loses the housing, the services can continue, or if a client refuses services they can continue to be housed.

4. Recovery is an ongoing process – Housing can be the first step along the path to recovery. Recovery consists of multiple stages and relapse is a normal part of the recovery process.

5. Community integration is fundamental and preferred by most participants, as opposed to creating institutionalized settings for independent living (Tsemberis 2010).

The Pathways to Housing program utilizes an Assertive Community Treatment model (ACT), however it designs the support service to be in line with the wishes of the consumer. ACT teams are community based and available 24 hours a day, seven days a week. Their services are open-ended and there is no requirement for individuals to graduate from the program. The ACT team can provide comprehensive services such as case management, vocational counseling, nursing services, psychiatry, peer support and crisis intervention (Tsemberis & Eisenberg 2000; Tsemberis et al. 2004). This model includes outreach to neighbors, property managers and landlords to help resolve conflicts and promote housing stabilization. While Pathways to Housing holds up the importance of consumer choice in regard to treatment, as well as individualizing and thereby shaping the support services offered, admittance to the program is conditional upon the person accepting payee-ship and a connection with a housing support service. The Pathways to Housing program provides sponsored-based housing and is therefore responsible for securing the rent from the program participant to pay the landlord. The advantage of partial guardianship or securing a payee to manage client finances is that the sub-leased tenant's rent is virtually guaranteed. However, there are some folks without homes who have a great deal of difficulty relinquishing direct control over their money and this could become a barrier to successfully housing a subset of the chronically homeless population. Overall, housing retention rates have been impressive. A two year study showed that 88% of Housing First participants in the Pathways to Housing program retained their housing (Tsemberis et al. 2004). Even after four years, housing retention rates remained higher in the Pathways to Housing program than those reported in the control group of those housed through traditional continuum of care programs (75% and 48% respectively). However, Tsemberis (2010, p. 52) notes that while Housing First may end homelessness, it does not cure psychiatric disability, addiction, or poverty. This underlines the importance of helping folks to address their economic status, as well as the importance of developing pathways to needed healthcare. A pretreatment approach, which is highlighted next via the REACH Housing First model, is an effective way of offering treatment alternatives.

REACH Housing First

Throughout the Western MA area, we have developed the Regional Engagement and Assessment of Chronically Homeless Housing First Program (REACH). This program not only attaches affordable housing options directly to outreach workers, but directly involves the outreach workers in the provision of ongoing support services to newly housed individuals. This is a relationship-centered model that supports transitions to needed housing, resources and services. Other important tasks for outreach staff include providing advocacy with landlords, as well as rapid response to any issue that may threaten safety and/or permanent housing. The need for rapid response falls under four basic categories:

1. Non-payment of rent
2. Conflict with neighbors

3. Destruction of property

4. Personal safety of tenant

If a person were once again to experience homelessness due to eviction or prematurely leaving their apartment, the Homeless Outreach process can easily resume. However, hopefully now the client and the team have good rapport and can work together toward more stable housing. Lessons learned from the previous attempt at housing can bring about greater stability.

The same pretreatment approach used to promote successful outreach can also be used to continue the work with newly housed individuals. This means that the residential outreach support services should continue to emphasize the basic pretreatment principles of relationship formation, common language construction, support the process of transition to needed resources and services, promote safety through harm reduction and crisis intervention, as well as facilitate positive change (Levy, 2000). Whether or not a particular Housing First program is run as a scattered site or congregate living model, it is essential that the support service component is well developed and responsive to the immediate needs of the tenant, landlord and neighbors. This also means providing the right level and intensity of support services based on the willingness and needs of the individual.

As noted in *Homeless Narratives & Pretreatment Pathways* (Levy, 2010), the following are the four core principles of the REACH Housing First program.

1. **The Relationship is Central & Ongoing**
   It is the relationship that is the jump off point to all services. The goal is to develop communication that feels safe, promotes trust and respects autonomy. The relationship transcends the immediate environment of shelter/ streets or residence, promoting successful transitions.

2. **Client is Ready for a Housing Focus**
   The hallmark of REACH and Pretreatment is to "get where the client is at." In other words, we accept that the client is always ready, so we must adjust by utilizing pretreatment strategies based on engagement and ecological considerations, common language construction, as well as promoting safety and facilitating change. Outreach staff offer homeless individuals housing as readily as offering

treatment, depending on client interest.

3. **Eligibility is Broad-Based and Inclusive**
   Chronic homelessness and lack of access to affordable housing with support services are the only qualifying criteria. A determination of eligibility for the program is based on functioning and access issues, rather than diagnosis (best fit/not exact match). This dissolves the barrier of first achieving eligibility to a particular system of care (i.e., Department of Mental Health, Department of Developmental Services, Statewide Head Injury Program, etc.), prior to getting housed with support services.

4. **The REACH Team Facilitates Transitions & Housing Stabilization**
   The outreach worker has direct access to affordable housing options and can therefore support transition to a residence, as well as ongoing support services.

Further, the outreach worker continues the work of housing stabilization by utilizing the advantages of an established positive relationship and common language, rather than immediately taking on the challenge of transitioning the client to new staff. This includes following a Psychiatric Rehabilitation approach (Anthony, 1990). The process involves developing needed supports, skills, and indicated environmental modifications to assure client safety and successful transition to a residence, as well as providing advocacy and mediation services with landlords. The long term objective is to promote housing stabilization by successfully connecting clients with community based supports, resources and services including indicated treatment for medical, mental health, and addiction issues.

This program has been adopted by the Western MA Region and has become a standard and highlighted component (All Roads Lead Home, 2008, p. 23) of the Pioneer Valley's plan to end chronic homelessness. It provides outreach, intensive case management, and has successfully housed unsheltered chronically homeless individuals who have historically lacked access to affordable housing and support services. Over a 5 year period, this program has shown a better than 85% housing retention rate. This is remarkable when you consider that 94 percent of its residents presented with co-occurring issues of severe mental illness and addiction, along with a major medical condition (tri-morbidity) and averaged more than 8 years of homelessness. The success of this program was a main contributor to a significant reduction in street homelessness throughout the city of Springfield, MA.

Safe Havens

Arguably, Safe Haven Programs and Pathways to Housing were among the earliest forms of Housing First. In 1992, Congress added an amendment to the Stewart B. McKinney Homeless Assistance Act, which included a provision for the creation of Safe Havens. According to Title IV, Subtitle D of the McKinney Act:

> A Safe Haven is a form of supportive housing that serves hard-to-reach homeless persons with severe mental illness who are on the street and have been unable or unwilling to participate in supportive services (SAMHSA-National Homeless Resource Center, 1997).

I classify Safe Haven Projects as Housing First because they primarily target unsheltered, chronically homeless individuals with major mental illnesses and do not demand treatment as prerequisite to accessing a residence. This is a shared residence with a small group of participants. Residential staff is on site and available 24/7 to provide support services. The length of stay is open ended, not time limited. There has been some debate (via HUD circles) whether or not to classify Safe Havens as permanent residences or to make them unique as neither transitional nor permanent. Regardless of the official classification, residents are welcome to stay as long as necessary before considering treatment and/or other permanent housing alternatives. The model is considered to be low demand/high expectation, meaning that there are not a lot of rules and/or demands put on clients, yet the hope is for the residents to get comfortable and to eventually work on achievable goals that may help them to move on to needed mental health treatment and alternative housing options. This model is completely in line with a pretreatment approach of an outreach and engagement process that is careful and respectful of the client's sense of safety, trust, and autonomy. The intake process for a Safe Haven program is interwoven with attempts to further engage the client and so staff could benefit from being trained on the basic stages of engagement and common language construction. Supporting transitions into the Safe Haven, as well as building bridges and pathways to treatment and other housing alternatives are also the common pretreatment goals of both Safe Haven staff and outreach workers.

Over the past 20 years or so, I have been fortunate to work with four different Safe Haven programs located throughout Massachusetts. All of them were small programs (no more than 12 residents) that have been effective at serving disaffiliated unsheltered homeless individuals with severe mental illnesses. Lacey's Narrative, as presented in Chapter 6, is but one of many examples of how a Safe Haven program can lead to a successful outcome. As someone who has provided outreach to unsheltered, homeless individuals with major disabilities, I know that having access to Safe Havens can be a godsend for those most in need. So it is a bit perplexing as to why HUD recently eliminated federal funding for new Safe Haven programs.

Funding C-SPECH Housing First Services

One of the more exciting developments in Massachusetts is that Medicaid (Mass Health via the Mass Behavioral Health Plan) is now allowing Housing First case management and outreach services to be directly billed for reimbursement. This is because several Housing First pilot programs throughout Massachusetts have demonstrated that affordable housing plus support services targeted to chronically homeless individuals directly lead to healthcare savings. Credit should be given to MHSA (Massachusetts Housing and Shelter Alliance, 2008), which, under the direction of Joseph Finn, provided relentless advocacy paired with the latest research data to get this and other Housing First programs funded throughout the Commonwealth. This particular initiative uses the acronym C-SPECH, which stands for Community Support Program for People Experiencing Chronic Homelessness. Fortunately, program designers understood that chronically homeless individuals may pose some significant challenges in regard to keeping appointments with housing support staff. So instead of billing for individual service hours based on actual services rendered, we are able to bill for each day that a Housing First Resident remains in the C-SPECH program, which amounts to a small daily reimbursement rate. This affords us the opportunity to spend some time with engagement and re-engagement services on an outreach basis, as opposed to having to end a Housing First support service due to a client missing 2 or 3 consecutive appointments.

I currently manage a small C-SPECH program and our staff have worked hand and hand with the PATH outreach program to identify chronically homeless clients who are in need of both affordable housing and ongoing housing support services. Together we have successfully placed these clients and utilized a pretreatment guide to promote housing stabilization. This is evidenced by a greater than 85% housing retention rate over a two year period of time. By pairing chronically homeless individuals who have billable health insurance with affordable housing units, we are able to fund dedicated housing first support staff. This model has achieved an integration of Housing First with standardized healthcare benefits. Mass Behavioral Health Plan staff should be applauded for their willingness to think out of the box and fund proven approaches for reducing chronic homelessness and related healthcare costs. More innovative Housing First programs with secure funding streams are needed far and wide, so we can continue our march forward with providing needed services to those who are most at risk.

Conclusion

Housing First is not a one size fits all formula and there are many different types of Housing First programs throughout the USA, Canada, and beyond. Among the keys to success are the ability to individualize and the flexibility of offered services. Housing First programs do a good job of meeting a combination of people's needs and wants, while attempting to facilitate positive change. Much like the Safe Haven model, staff work from the premise of low demand/ high expectation. Different Housing First models have been reviewed to underline the fact that Housing First is not simply about giving homeless people a place to stay. The variations discussed here target those who are at highest risk and the support service component, in its various forms and permutations, is a necessary and essential part of the model. Overall, many studies have compared housing retention among Housing First participants to people enrolled in traditional continuum of care programs. Housing First programs that were reflective of the Pathways to Housing design showed higher levels of housing retention (Tsemberis & Eisenberg 2000; Gulcur et al. 2003; Tsemberis et al. 2004; Stefanic & Tsemberis 2007; Pearson et al. 2009; Tsai et al. 2010). The research results have been encouraging in regard to consumer satisfaction, length of stay, and cost effectiveness.

A pretreatment perspective integrated with the Housing First model guides us toward providing not only the right types of accommodations, supports, and housing, but also provides guidance in working with a person's ideas, values, and overall narrative in an effort to redefine their sense of place within the community. The goal is to promote safety and housing stabilization, while developing meaningful structure and supportive relationships for this disenfranchised homeless population. Our goals and challenges should include helping individuals to feel more at home and part of the community in which they live. Dedicated staff and supervision are needed to see it through from the stage of program development to effective field practice. The next chapter highlights the interplay between Homeless Outreach, Housing First, and supervision.

Chapter 10 – Julio's Narrative: The Trials & Tribulations of Housing First

> "Every night they try to break into my apartment, but I am on to them. I can hear what they are planning through the walls!"
>
> – Julio

Outreach & Engagement

Julio was a bilingual (Spanish & English), 34 years old Hispanic male who grew up in Puerto Rico and then moved to Western Massachusetts to stay with his uncle. One morning Julio awoke to discover that his uncle had passed away and ended up leaving the residence, but had no place to go. Frightened and disoriented from his uncle's sudden death and his newly found homeless state, he resorted to camping in the woods. Without anyone to turn to, he became chronically homeless before he eventually ended up staying at a local homeless shelter.

Julio was good with his hands and had been able to work periodically in construction, but invariably left these jobs due to conflicts with co-workers. He reported occasional marijuana usage, but denied any other current alcohol or drug use or abuse. He presented with paranoid ideation and was often highly suspicious of people's intent, which led to a number of direct threats and highly charged confrontations with others. He had a long history of denying the severity of his mental illness and refused treatment. Our outreach clinician who had a master's degree in clinical psychology and was adept at conversational Spanish successfully engaged with Julio. The outreach counselor also brought with him an appreciation of Puerto Rican culture due to his multiple visits to the island and this resonated well with Julio. In fact, after their first couple of meetings, Julio declared, "You're the only white man I can trust!" The worker felt deeply honored by Julio's statement, while remaining sensitive to the mistrust that a person of a minority group may experience when dealing with people of the white majority who are often in positions of power.

The outreach counselor and I met weekly for clinical supervision. Initially, the supervision process helped the counselor to apply the stages of common language construction to his work. This assisted the worker and Julio in developing a playground of language that reframed the concept of "Mental Illness" to include feeling unsafe, perpetual conflict with others, and a sense of mistrust due to past bad experiences. Julio understood this to be a barrier to his maintaining employment and therefore agreed to apply for disability benefits via social security. He later qualified for benefits and this strengthened his engagement with the outreach worker, though he remained distrustful of others and continued to refuse any type of formal treatment. Nevertheless, his establishment of an income, his continued engagement with the outreach team, and a willingness to be housed met the primary criteria to enter our Housing First program.

Housing First Placement: Crisis Intervention and Supporting Transitions

Shortly thereafter, Julio moved into an affordable apartment and received REACH outreach services. This meant that the same outreach worker who had established a trusting relationship and a well-developed playground of language with Julio now provided Housing First counseling and stabilization services. The outreach counselor was an extremely dedicated employee with excellent counseling skills, though relatively new to the concept of Housing First. He was a bit puzzled on how to help someone with acute untreated mental illness consisting of severe paranoid symptoms to successfully live with neighbors in a permanent affordable housing setting. As it turned out, there was some cause for concern because Julio had major conflicts with the other tenants and became quite delusional. He believed that his neighbors were a direct threat to his own health and safety. Julio said, "Every night they try to break into my apartment, but I am on to them. I can hear what they are planning through the walls!" On the one hand Julio had shown himself to be a capable tenant in terms of paying rent and taking care of his apartment. On the other, he increasingly felt that his safety was jeopardized and had responded by becoming more threatening toward others. Fortunately, Julio continued to have a good relationship with the Housing First counselor and the worker was very open and responsive to our supervision, which included learning from my past successes with housing and stabilizing clients who present with acute psychiatric issues, while refusing treatment.

Over a period of one year, the counselor was able to stay engaged with Julio, while working closely with the mental health crisis team to have him hospitalized on three different occasions. Each time Julio was transitioned back to his apartment, he would do well for a couple of months before becoming increasingly paranoid. This took a toll on neighbors, the landlord, the counselor, and Julio. I did my best to support and supervise the counselor's work through several crisis episodes. One of the counselor's main tasks was to meet with all impacted parties to help assure their sense of safety and control. In addition, the counselor provided Julio with the opportunity to voluntarily move to a quieter and more secure residence. Julio, with a sense of urgency, immediately responded, "If you can get me a new place, I'll move there as soon as possible. In the meantime, I'll do whatever I have to do to defend myself." The offer to move was consistent with Julio's impulse for flight and he saw this as a way to relieve stress and restore his sense of safety and well-being.

Approximately two weeks later, we were able to find an affordable apartment in a building with fewer tenants. It was a less stimulating environment that was consistent with Julio's needs and provided a natural transition point for exploring what Julio learned from his most recent tenancy. This lead to the counselor and Julio jointly formulating new crisis-safety plans, coping strategies, and potential referrals to other needed services. Supervision played a critical role in helping the counselor to time his interventions to be in line with the appropriate stages of Engagement, Common Language Construction, and Change. Early on, it was not unusual for the counselor to offer treatment options, when Julio was clearly pre-contemplative and not ready to contract for additional services. Instead the worker needed to focus on strengthening engagement and to establish goals that were relevant to Julio, yet could eventually be bridged through a common language to treatment related services.

Managing Crisis and Learning Opportunities

One positive result was that Julio clearly stated his displeasure at being involuntarily hospitalized, so the counselor and he were able to develop a plan to try and avoid that outcome. The worker and Julio explored the discrepancy between Julio's wish to remain out of the hospital and safe, with his unwillingness to even try a medication to reduce stress and improve his ability to tolerate others. Due to a strong rapport with the counselor and by applying the psychiatric rehabilitation principle of negotiation, Julio agreed to take psychotropic medications as a limited time experiment to see whether or not it helped to reduce stress and confrontations with others. In addition, we instituted a backup plan that utilized a voluntary mental health respite stay, as opposed to involuntary inpatient care.

Another idea that had traction with Julio was to add a day activity by referring him to a local Clubhouse program that served folks with major mental illnesses. Julio showed interest in this program because it focused on work and social activities, rather than illness and treatment. Julio possessed good painting and carpentry skills, and the local Clubhouse was able to get him temporary work in these areas. This established a clear pathway to greater housing stability and meaningful structure, but his progress was not completely linear. It took more of the form of a dialectical relationship; slowly over time, repeated events of crisis were matched with the new opportunities for learning. As long as the outreach counselor remained engaged with Julio and was available to follow up with inpatient, respite, and crisis workers, things continued to spiral forward. Eventually, after one more hospitalization, a respite stay, and yet another move, Julio was able to show clear progress and long-term housing stability (more than 2 years housed). He was also able to participate in treatment by taking prescribed medications, used the mental health respite program as needed, and became a highly involved Clubhouse member and well liked neighbor.

Julio's Story Revisited: Pretreatment Guide for Supervision

There were three main areas where supervision contributed to the counselor's success:

1. It restored optimism and reinforced the possibility of positive results.
2. It helped the counselor to embrace points of crisis and transition as opportunities to facilitate positive change.

3. Pretreatment Principles of care were jointly reviewed and used as a guide for the counselor's case assessment/ intervention and advocacy/referral to needed resources and services.

Supervision initially focused on the puzzle of how to best serve someone who adamantly refused treatment, while struggling with significant paranoid ideation. Since the counselor was relatively new to a Housing First approach, the client's refusal of treatment and initial conflicts with neighbors quickly diminished his hopes. The key for my success as a supervisor was to engage well with the counselor and together we worked on development of pretreatment pathways that the client could take. Even though these pathways were completely dependent upon the work between the counselor and client, I facilitated this creative process by coaching the counselor on how to apply pretreatment principles. It was important for us to embrace this work with a sense of possibility and purpose, as opposed to feeling that we were in the midst of an impossible task. In this particular case, this was done on many levels. First and foremost, the worker did not have a firsthand frame of reference for what can be achieved via Housing First for people with untreated mental illnesses.

As a supervisor, I have found that sharing Housing First success stories of clients who have faced similar obstacles is a powerful way to restore the optimism that is essential to facilitating positive outcomes. I often refer to these narratives as the many miracles we've experienced along the way. This same process was also practiced via group supervision where other team members shared their success stories, while reviewing the intricacies of their work with formerly hard to reach homeless individuals with major mental illnesses, addictions and medical issues who historically refused treatment. These were the same folks that other providers had given up on and had advised us to do the same. Yet time after time, a pretreatment approach matched with affordable housing had demonstrated its effectiveness at helping people with long homeless histories who were untreated and highly symptomatic.

One of the more difficult tasks is for our workers to embrace crisis. It is all too easy to shy away from these opportunities, even though they can be the impetus for positive change. Our work with Julio contained many points of crisis and each hospitalization resulted in periods of treatment along with the chance to consider how best to transition him back to his apartment. Each round of crisis required supervisory input to guide the referral and advocacy with the crisis team in order to facilitate a voluntary or involuntary mental health evaluation to determine the need for inpatient care. Successful advocacy was dependent upon understanding the world of the crisis worker and presenting in a common clinical-behavioral language that resonated well. On a systems level, the basic principles of engagement, common language development, and supporting transitions were instrumental considerations to promote a positive result via the crisis team and with inpatient staff. The worker was able to stay well engaged and continued to share a common language with Julio, so they were able to discuss what led to each hospitalization, as well as actively participate in discharge planning with the hospital social worker. This eventually led to Julio being more open to psychotropic medications, as well as strengthening his current coping skills, and considering a mental health respite as a viable alternative to inpatient care. The great rapport between the worker and Julio made this possible. Supervision played a key role in that it helped the worker to envision positive outcomes, manage numerous crisis episodes, and provided guidance with bridging the language from Julio's world so he could more fully embrace viable treatment options.

Chapter 11 – Supervision: Pretreatment Applications, Staff Support and Sharing Stories

> "Optimism is the faith that leads to achievement; nothing can be done without hope."
> – Helen Keller (1903)

Pretreatment Applications

The central question for supervision is, *How can we help our staff provide quality outreach based services?* Our main objective is to form a trusting and supportive relationship with staff members, while upholding and facilitating the application of their various strengths and aptitudes to their work. Over the many years of doing supervision, I have found that the most successful employees were unique individuals who found meaning in their vocation. They had such a strong sense of mission that helping the homeless became an essential part of their identity. It is important to help facilitate the *meaning making* process for staff, and to respect their individuality by giving voice to their stories. This encompasses the telling of their own work narratives, as well as hearing the many client stories that are encountered and formed over the many weeks and months of outreach. In many ways, the challenges of working with staff mirror our work with clients. On the one hand, the five principles of pretreatment can serve as a guide toward developing positive and productive relationships with staff. On the other, our goal is to successfully pass on the basic principles and underpinnings of a pretreatment philosophy to staff, while providing ongoing support, clinical consultation and direction regarding appropriate resources and services.

The five pretreatment principles discussed throughout this book can help facilitate positive change on both individual and system levels of care. A supervisor with an understanding of a pretreatment paradigm and its applications can be an effective guide. Outreach counselors and Housing First staff working with hard to reach untreated populations can benefit from the opportunity for regular case review and feedback. When faced with chronic and acute issues, it is easy for staff to feel frustrated and to lose hope. The supervisor needs to provide an experienced perspective and facilitate a sense of optimism and equilibrium. This requires sharing past challenging cases, situations and successes. By utilizing pretreatment principles mixed with past and present case narratives, we can help staff to discover productive pathways for helping. When working with persons who had experienced long-term homelessness, addressing their safety and immediacy needs was often the doorway for promoting the change process. Ultimately it is the supervisor's job to provide guidance, boost morale and instill hope. I can recall several occasions when direct care staff were beginning to give up on aiding hard to serve clients. In response, we explored the application of different pretreatment strategies and then proceeded to discuss potential pathways for helping.

A worker and supervisor can jointly ponder a number of questions in an effort to reinvigorate the work with the hardest to reach folks. Some of these questions are:

- What stage of engagement are you and the client at, and are you focusing the work on stage-relevant tasks?

- Are you well engaged with a good rapport, or does more work need to be done to gain client trust prior to working on goals?

- Are you both working from a common frame of reference or does this need to be developed further via stages of common language development?

- What's the client's story and what does he or she value or find meaningful... what are the particular words and phrases used to express this?

- Are there current safety risks to you or the client? If so, how can we address these risks to minimize potential harm?

- Can you visualize a potential pathway for helping the client?

- Have you contracted for services and jointly defined goals to be worked on?

- Do these goals resonate well in the client's world, or does more work need to be done to interpret, reframe, or redefine goals via the client's language?

- What are the client's strengths and challenges and how do they relate to the development of a potential pretreatment pathway to housing, resources, and services?

- What are the systemic barriers? Are the barriers connected to the client's limitations or challenges, or are they systemic demands that are either unreasonable or don't apply to the particular circumstance? How can we resolve, accommodate or work around these barriers via advocacy, applying reasonable accommodation laws, and/or modifying the environment, supports and client behavior?

- How can we support transitions to new ideas, people, environments, and services?

- Should we incorporate some forms of desensitization strategies for supporting new transitions?

- What new opportunities do a particular transition and/or crisis provide? How do our interventions reflect these opportunities, while upholding safety?

- What's the full list of services and helping resources that is a good match for the client's particular needs and goals?

Staff Supervision: Boundary Issues and Workers' Reactions

Outreach and engagement practices with chronically homeless persons are purposely informal in nature. This can lead to difficulties in attaining and maintaining appropriate boundaries with clients. This is one of the core challenges throughout the stages of outreach and engagement. Supervision can be used to reflect on thorny issues such as when does it make sense to feed dependency needs, as well as providing a more in-depth consideration of how to form and reinforce boundaries in various homeless venues. The formation of boundaries based on the outreach-counseling developmental model (refer back to Table 5 on p. 83) and the five clinical principles of pretreatment, was first presented in the book *Homeless Narratives & Pretreatment Pathways* (2010) and is reprised here for your consideration. Clearly, the engagement process begins informally, and dependency needs are fed during the pre-engagement stage in order to foster initial communication. During this phase, we may offer needed items to clients, and communication begins more on the clients' terms, as we seek permission to enter and understand their world. We are challenged by the process of developing boundaries because we don't have a clear set of office-based rules and duties (Office Culture) to guide us. As communication becomes more welcome, we enter the engagement stage and it is during this stage that we begin to define boundaries by introducing and reviewing our roles as outreach counselors and what duties that can potentially entail. During the engagement stage, we foster a common language with the aim of defining mutually acceptable goals that can guide our work into the contracting stage. Upon contracting with clients, our roles and duties are further defined, clarified, and reinforced.

During the contract implementation phase, we are providing a counseling relationship that supports client ownership of goals and initiative for positive change. During this phase, supporting transitions to housing and/or treatment related services (i.e., day programs, Community Health & MH clinics, addiction programs, etc.) are critical. We may need to temporarily increase our level of support to promote the bridging process and adaptation to these new environments, people, and ideas. Upon entering the stage of termination, it is best if our roles and boundaries are redefined in conjunction with the client's engagement and contracting with other providers. Over time the outreach-counseling relationship comes to an end. However, if the client were to re-experience homelessness, we may provide short-term intervention and redirection to housing and support services. Both the client and counselor experience issues of loss, which can result in the counselor and client overreaching newly defined boundaries (role confusion).

An additional consideration is that crisis can occur during any phase of the outreach-counseling process. An individual in crisis is having difficulty with his or her adaptive functioning in critical areas necessary for self-care and is struggling with acute issues. Crisis intervention dictates that the counselor takes a more directive stance, inclusive of feeding dependency to assure safety. Finally, a harm reduction model can further guide our work. Needed items such as clothes, food, blankets, and even clean needles may be offered at different stages of the counseling process, and apart from crisis situations, to help assure future safety, and/or reduce the risk of harm to self or others. Arguably this may also feed dependency rather than self-sufficiency, but it is at times necessary to *promote safety* (pretreatment principle) via both harm reduction and crisis intervention strategies.

Outreach work to under-served populations can and does elicit powerful feelings and behaviors from the counselor such as wanting to save or take care of clients, trying to dictate or control outcomes, and becoming overly authoritative or angry with other providers, etc. It is important that the worker has the opportunity to voice and reflect upon these feelings and behaviors; otherwise the counselor's judgment and interventions may be compromised or become ineffective. Particular phases of relationship formation are apt to elicit these types of responses. During the pre-engagement phase, the worker often struggles with the impulse to "save" the client from danger, or his or her own fears of the homeless world. The impulse to "save" may cause the worker to be overly aggressive and thereby take unwarranted safety risks, or push the work too quickly without attention to the client's need for an incremental transition. An overly fearful tendency may cause the worker to proceed too cautiously, thereby missing the opportunity to engage with reachable clients. The goal of pre-engagement is to establish a sense of safety via an initial welcomed communication, which will hopefully lead to further engagement.

Throughout the phase of *engagement,* the worker may struggle with feelings of wanting to take care of the client, or with the belief that a homeless person must take responsibility for his or her own situation. If either tendency is taken to an extreme, it will interfere with both boundary definition and role development between worker and client. The challenge of the engagement phase is to establish an *ongoing* communication that promotes trust and respects autonomy, while further defining roles and boundaries. Similarly, throughout the stage of contracting, the worker may struggle with being too directive or fostering complete client autonomy without providing adequate guidance. Either of these tendencies, taken to an extreme, can reinforce a homeless person's sense of shame and guilt, rather than promote independence. The challenge is to facilitate the client's exploration of possible goals and interests, so that he or she can experience a sense of autonomy and initiative throughout the process of contract development. This type of analysis can also be done regarding an array of relationship-based issues that arise throughout the outreach-counseling process including but not limited to, issues of shame, guilt, anger, grief and loss. Supervision, whether it be peer supervision or with a clinical supervisor, provides the sense of grounding and centering needed to help workers stay on task. Our objective is to find pretreatment pathways to success, which are invariably built upon a trusting relationship and a common language between client and worker.

Supporting Transitions, Sharing Stories & Common Pitfalls

Outreach counselors bear witness to trauma and loss as a normal part of their workday. It is the supervisor's responsibility to provide a supportive forum for frontline staff to process potentially traumatic field experiences. Peer support groups and 1:1 supervision are particularly effective for providing the self-help that is required for sustaining a sense of balance and connection, rather than feeling overwhelmed, isolated, and vicariously traumatized. The work we are asking our staff to do is very demanding and emotionally drain-ing. It takes a broad range of skills and adequate support to do it successfully. Proper supervision can make a positive difference in the quality of outreach counseling services delivered. Group and individual supervision provides the opportunity to utilize a pretreat-ment approach for reflecting on cases, including assessment and intervention considerations.

It is important that outreach counselors are provided with an appropriate venue to tell their stories. They've gone on countless journeys with the homeless persons they are trying to help, and have a great deal to share with one another. Much can be learned whether it is success stories, specific dilemmas, or traumatic experiences. Through this kind of sharing and feedback, outreach counselors can begin to balance their limitations with what is possible, and thereby achieve the sense of serenity and perspective required to continually do this work well. A culture of sharing and providing each other with support needs to be initially facilitated and reinforced by the supervisor. This includes establishing a group process where outreach workers become comfortable presenting cases, sharing grief and loss issues, as well as seeking support and consultation from team members. If we are to be successful in maintaining long-term highly qualified staff, then we need to provide the opportunities for high quality 1:1 supervision and peer group support. This is essential because the effectiveness of a pretreatment program is ultimately dependent upon staff being sensitive and responsive to a broad range of issues and challenges.

One of the central tasks of supervision is to support transitions. Whether it is the orientation of a new employee, or when someone is leaving their job, the supervisor plays a critical role toward facilitating this process. The heart of outreach counseling is relationship based, so proper orientation and termination will directly impact both the team and the clients we serve. The more we build a culture of team work and support, the easier it is to involve other team members in training new staff, or providing coverage during vacations or after a worker has left employment. A new employee joining our team is oriented through one-on-one and group supervision, as well as provided with important literature on homelessness, a listing of area services and resources, and given an array of policies and procedures to help organize their work. My organization even goes as far as to provide a week of extensive training inclusive of reviewing Health Insurance Portability and Accountability Act (HIPPA) and mandated reporting standards, corporate compliance procedures and even a review of potential boundary violations and vital counseling skills such as Suicide Assessment and Motivational Interviewing techniques.

Invariably, employees learn the most from orientation activities, when they go on outreach tours with different team members and can witness the work up close ranging from initial engagement strategies to the client referral process and supporting transitions to new services and resources. As a rule, I like to send new workers on 3 separate outreach missions where they can shadow highly skilled veteran employees. Immediately afterward, we meet to debrief and review whatever questions they may have. This process simultaneously strengthens the team, trains a new worker, and sets the table for effective ongoing supervision. As this and other examples illustrate, as a supervisor it is important to balance general training protocols with effective individualization of the supervisory process to better meet the needs and strengths of our workers.

Common pitfalls can be mitigated by understanding that assessment is truly a dynamic process. An intervention that may be an important harm reduction strategy at one phase of the engagement or change process may be enabling during a different phase. This is part of exposing the myth that the worker should never work harder than the client. The reality is that in order to be successful with Housing First, outreach, and a pretreatment approach, we will sometimes be required to work much harder than the client. This is particularly true during the early stages of engagement, as well as during crisis and transition points with people who are refusing treatment, yet experience major mental illnesses and addictions. At the same time, we need to be savvy in our interventions, so they are congruent with the particular stage of engagement, common language construction, and change that is most relevant to the client's circumstance. Supervision can help workers to focus on the application of these different stage-based models in order to more effectively "get where the client is at." The nature of these stage based models, whether it be in regard to phases of change, engagement, or common language development, is that they provide a road map and with it direction and hope for improvement.

It is important to note that this chapter does not claim to present the full breadth of supervisory activities, nor is it meant to be an in-depth guide to the process of supervision. Further topics to explore could be a full review of transference/counter transference issues and the development of particular counseling skill sets, facilitating proper data collection and the integration of new technologies with our practice, etc. What it does provide is an understanding of how a pretreatment paradigm has diverse applications and how its general principles can be applied to the process of supervision. I am confident and have learned through firsthand experience that this pretreatment guide effectively supports and provides consultation to the meaningful work of Homeless Outreach and Housing First staff.

Chapter 12 – Conclusion

> "Any idea upon which we can ride, so to speak; any idea that will carry us prosperously from any one part of our experience to any other part, linking things satisfactorily, working securely, simplifying, saving labor... is true instrumentally."
>
> – William James (1907)

A pretreatment guide based on universal principles of care has been presented and applied to Homeless Outreach and Housing First activities. This project is unique in that it presents intricate and detailed stories of outreach to those who have experienced long-term and/or multiple episodes of homelessness. The reader is given a ground view of the outreach process and the numerous challenges of engaging with the most vulnerable and disaffiliated members of our communities. This includes but is not limited to the complexities of assisting couples, youth, and unaccompanied adults with co-occurring disorders of substance abuse and mental illness.

The Client Centered Pragmatism of Pretreatment

A pretreatment approach is versatile and respects the individuality of both workers and clients. It is not a specific recipe for helping, but rather a general guide that encourages creativity through the dynamic interplay of relationship-based work and common language development. It is focused on people's stories and developing a sense of authorship and responsibility for bringing about positive change. Its only demand is that the worker follows five general principles of care, while remaining optimistic and dedicated as a facilitator, rather than an authority. Drawing off Narrative Psychology, we respect that the client is the true expert on his or her own world. A pretreatment approach does not concern itself with what is technically treatment or Housing First because it is founded on client-centered pragmatism. The main concern is what works or what is useful for the client. This frees the worker from established modes of intervention and preprogrammed responses in favor of individualized goals, strategies and plans that resonate well with the individual. We've learned that being too prescriptive limits possibilities and writes off many of the people who need our help the most. Therefore, we are always concerned about "getting where the clients are at" and bridging them to needed resources and services, rather than determining that they are "not ready" or ineligible. Our work flows into the person's world with the current of an individual's values, language and sensibilities. Our hope is to join with clients and transition them to the housing and/or treatment essential to their overall sense of health and well-being.

Homeless Outreach & Housing First: Resolution of Conflicting Dualities

The five principles of pretreatment, complemented by extensive case narratives, provide direction and insight to the daily challenges faced by Homeless Outreach and Housing First staff. This book has closely examined the interconnection of Homeless Outreach and Housing First activities by demonstrating that the basic tasks of outreach and engagement remain the same whether it is on the streets or in a Housing First residence. Either way, the issue is how to work most effectively with people who have experienced the trauma of homelessness, as well as acute or chronic symptoms of untreated major mental illnesses and/or addictions. A pretreatment perspective brings together substance abuse and mental health treatment philosophies, while also being a trauma informed practice. This is done by integrating change model and motivational interviewing strategies with Narrative Psychology and client-centered, goal driven approaches.

Perhaps the greatest strength of pretreatment is that it can serve as a type of meta-language or guide to integrate potential conflicting dualities. There is often tension between clinical approaches to mental health vs. addictions, or with social justice strategies vs. clinical interventions, or even between the approaches of Homeless Outreach vs. residential services. A pretreatment perspective finds the interconnections between these worlds by utilizing universal principles of care that are accepted by interdisciplinary staff and practiced in a wide range of settings. Most folks can agree and the research has shown the importance of building client-centered relationships, improving communication by forming a common language, and supporting transitions to new environments, as well as promoting safety and facilitating the process of positive change. This forms a powerful approach to service delivery that can bring together advocates, clinicians, case managers, program planners, and policy makers toward embracing the specific roles they can play, and a common frame of reference in achieving the shared objective of ending or significantly reducing chronic homelessness.

Goals & Future Challenges

We have discussed the relevance of a pretreatment perspective in regard to the process of Homeless Outreach and housing stabilization. This does not suggest that other factors are less important, or irrelevant. In fact, interagency partnerships and community group efforts are instrumental to the development of an adequate safety net, and helps to identify and house those who are most in need. This is our best hope for maximizing system-wide efforts in order to protect existing resources, and promote access to housing and support services, while developing new innovative programs. Nationwide Homeless Outreach initiatives and the Housing First movement have made some inroads in reducing chronic homelessness and its significant fiscal and moral costs. However, when we look at the societal ill of homelessness and the indignities that people without homes continue to endure, it is apparent that a great deal of unfinished work needs to be accomplished. Overall, there has been very little written about the *intricacies* of utilizing a pretreatment approach with couples, youth and unaccompanied adults with co-occurring disorders.

I hope that I have furthered the conversation by presenting the challenges of Homeless Outreach and Housing First through the art of storytelling, thoughtful reflection, and considering relevant theory and research. I know that the work with youth and couples is very rich and diverse, so we could certainly benefit by exploring new narratives and through careful study develop an array of best practices. Further, it is evident that we need to increase the number of accessible, affordable housing resources matched with flexible support services that can be tailored to meet the specific needs of homeless and formerly homeless individuals with disabilities. Finally, our outreach to people with and without homes is comprised of significant challenges such as stabilizing crises, developing skills and supports, facilitating the meaning making process, and building a sense of belonging to the community. A pretreatment guide for outreach workers and residential support staff is an essential and important contribution to these critical endeavors.

In closing, the goal of pretreatment is twofold. First, it is to join with individuals, couples and others who are most at risk, so we can construct pathways that lead to the world of crucial resources and support services. Second, we must build pathways from the world of services and resources to welcome those who are in such dire need. In many respects, this is my opening volley in the discussions of homeless couples and youth, while providing an in-depth account of how to apply pretreatment principles to a diverse range of people and situations. The narratives of Ronald, Lacey, Anthony, Julio, Janice and Michael have shown that a pretreatment guide to service delivery played an instrumental role for helping them to not only get housed, but also improved the quality of their lives by participating in needed healthcare services. This approach can potentially help many more if adopted by outreach workers, Housing First Staff, case managers, street physicians, and others.

As outreach workers, we carry the unenviable task of reminding the system of care that critical issues need to be addressed and that people's stability and perhaps even their lives can be at risk when we don't provide the care that a particular person or situation warrants. A pretreatment approach can empower our work toward greater individualization and a more sensitive response to client needs, while also building an advocacy language based on universal principles of care. I have shared my story throughout this book, while describing the variety of challenges and successes people without homes have experienced. I hope that its message can be heard and acted upon to make a meaningful difference in people's lives.

Appendix – Homelessness in America

The following article is an Interview Excerpt via the *Journal of Humanitarian Affairs*

Michell Spoden is the author of *Stricken Yet Crowned* (2011) and a reporter for the *Journal of Humanitarian Affairs* (online at www.GreenHeritageNews.com).

Despite having a team of American astronauts land on the moon more than four decades ago, America still has around a million homeless people, many of whom don't even have shelter and have to live on the streets. This situation calls for attention on a national level to alleviate the suffering of these people who are vulnerable to rough weather, accidents, crime, and all kinds of risks arising from the lack and comfort of a house to live in.

After reading an interview with Jay S. Levy, author of the books *Homeless Narratives & Pretreatment Pathways: From Words to Housing* and *Homeless Outreach & Housing First: Lessons Learned*, I contacted him for telling us more about important issues in housing for homeless people in the US. The following are my questions which Jay Levy answered by explaining, informing, and suggesting solutions to manage homelessness in America.

Michell: I recently read the interview[*] that you did with Ernest Dempsey in the Digital Journal entitled "Around 1.5 million homeless as US enters 2011". In the article you mention words such as Integrity, Collaboration, Advocacy, and Concerned Individuals. Can you tell me if you think there has been a shift since 2011 that has created better solutions to these issues? If so what are they? If not what are they?

Jay Levy: Where I live and work (Western MA), we've begun something called the REACH initiative, which stands for Regional

---

[*] http://digitaljournal.com/article/301929

Engagement and Assessment of Chronically Homeless-Housing First. We've constructed outreach teams that are directly connected to housing resources and support services that are enumerated and discussed via monthly REACH meetings. The REACH meetings have representatives of area housing and service providers and we actively match chronically homeless individuals of highest vulnerability via the vulnerability index (Research by Dr. James O'Connell and put forth by Common Ground†) to needed housing, support services, and other resources. This has resulted in us housing many high-risk individuals with major mental health, addiction, and medical issues. We've significantly reduced the unsheltered homeless population in Springfield, MA, as well as in other parts of Western MA. One of the important aspects of the program is how we support transitions to housing and the pretreatment approach that we utilize based on 5 principles of care:

1. Relationship Formation – Stages of Engagement: Develop trust and respect client autonomy.

2. Common Language Construction – Stages of common language development: Fostering good communication between worker and client.

3. Ecological Considerations – Supporting transition and adaptation to new ideas, environments, services, housing and treatment, etc.

4. Facilitating Change – via application of Change model and motivational interviewing.

5. Promoting Safety – via Harm Reduction and Crisis Intervention approaches.

Setting up new programs and bringing the proper resources and services to bear is only one part of the puzzle. The way we go about doing outreach and the type of support services we provide are critical to our success of permanently housing the most vulnerable among us. This is particularly challenging for folks who have experienced long-term homelessness and have struggled with addictions and major mental health issues.

When you experience the hard realities of homelessness and poverty, I know that it is easy to get discouraged and to think that

---

† http://www.jedc.org/forms/Vulnerability%20Index.pdf

people don't really care. However, every day I witness people trying to stem the tide of homelessness and making efforts to help people without homes successfully transition to new residences. One exciting example is Common Ground (www.commonground.org), which is an organization located in NYC that has created over 3,000 housing units with support services for chronically homeless individuals. They have shared their commonsense approach with others and have collaborated with various organizations across the country to spearhead a national campaign to house 100,000 chronically homeless individuals by the end of 2013.

Another organization by the name of Pathways to Housing (www.pathwaystohousing.org) has been successfully providing Housing First Programs since 1992. Dr. Sam Tsemberis is the founder of Pathways to Housing and he has been helping to set up new Housing First programs in many cities across the country, including NYC, Philadelphia, and Washington, DC. During 2011, he also published a guidebook entitled *Housing First Manual: The Pathways Model to End Homelessness for People with Mental Illness and Addiction*. Also the HEARTH Act has expanded the definition of homelessness to include a broader population inclusive of youth who are doubled up or couch surfing and women who have recently experienced domestic violence. In addition, the chronically homeless definition now includes families.

Broadening these definitions means that more folks will qualify for the aid they need and deserve, so things are moving in the right direction. At the same time, there are real concerns that I don't want to gloss over. Unemployment continues to hover around 8%, many folks don't make a decent living wage, and housing is not all that affordable. This is among the root causes of homelessness, and as a result, we have seen an increase in family homelessness, while we tread water to keep the numbers stable or slightly improving with homeless individuals and Veterans.

The national numbers on Veterans without homes have shown a small yet significant reduction over the past couple of years due to the influx of funds to support the Veterans Affairs Supportive Housing (VASH) program, which consists of a *subsidized housing voucher* matched with case management services for veterans without homes. In fact, homeless veterans may want to check with the local VA to see if VASH Vouchers are currently available in their region. On the flipside, we are bracing ourselves for the ramifications of two wars (Iraq & Afghanistan) and the inevitable fallout that these wars have and will bring: broken families, Post-Traumatic Stress syndrome, traumatic brain injury, and homelessness.

Michell: Do you also think that the local police departments should be better educated on how to mediate on these issues?

Jay: My short answer is yes, but I also believe that we should always look to what's been tried and what's already working before we try to fix it. In other words, some police departments have set up community policing programs, which consist of the police doing outreach, having an active presence in the community, and getting to know the people who live there. This means that the cop who patrols a particular area also builds relationships with landlords, businesses, the faith community, as well as people with and without homes. At the same time, I encourage my staff to do outreach to the police and to do our best to clearly explain our mission of helping the homeless and some of the inevitable difficulties that arise. This includes judgment-impaired behaviors that lead to violence and victimization, threats of suicide, as well as difficulties that can play out with landlords and hotel managers. Out in Western MA, we have set up quarterly meetings between police personnel, mental health crisis teams, and Homeless Outreach workers to discuss how we can help each other to respond better to crisis situations in the community.

I am a strong believer in utilizing engagement strategies with law enforcement, landlords, shelter managers, and other resources and services that people without homes may require. At the same time, it is extremely important that we remain independent from the police, town or city management, and other authorities. In the end, we are advocates for the homeless and impoverished, while having good relations with the power structure can facilitate getting what our clients need and deserve.

Technically, a cop can stick to a very narrow view of what he is there to do… namely enforce the law. However, from a community policing perspective, the role of the police is much broader than that and certainly could include understanding tenancy laws, advocating for tenant rights, crisis response and mediation between landlord and tenant to prevent an emergency—such as sudden homelessness—from occurring. In the end, much of our work is facilitated by the formation of positive relationships.

There are times when we encounter police who abuse their authority. On occasion, it is imbedded as part of the culture of an entire police department, but most often it is due to one bad cop, or a real lack of training on how to address behavioral health issues. Unfortunately, it is often the homeless and less fortunate who suffer the consequences. I am sadly reminded of the brutal killing of a homeless man with untreated schizophrenia named Thomas Kelly[‡]. He was suspected of burglarizing a car and a half dozen cops responded by repeatedly using a stun-gun to electroshock this unarmed man into submission. This resulted in Thomas dying from his Taser-inflicted injuries.

First and foremost, my sympathies go out to the family of Thomas Kelly. We are always concerned when the police are not given the proper training for de-escalating situations that involve people with major mental illnesses. Mental health training[§] paired with the input of psychiatric crisis teams can help the police to respond more effectively, thereby averting future tragedies. If we are serious about addressing issues of homelessness and major mental illness, it is essential that we provide ongoing outreach and affordable housing to those who are the most vulnerable among us, rather than criminalizing it. Ultimately, this is not only a moral issue, but will cost tax payers less, as well as save lives, if we provide proper training and enact the right policies.

Michell: Jay, this is very good to know and obviously a model for other police departments to follow.

There are so many people with disabilities who struggle to try and maintain their housing. Earlier I provided you with a case illustration of a gentleman with developmental issues who also is a collector of various items that he perceives as being essential toward establishing a future business. Can you reflect a bit on the issues of hoarding and the need for support services?

Jay Levy: A major challenge of housing stabilization is to deal with the negative impact of hoarding behaviors. When we apply a pretreatment approach, we always ask the question of how our words and actions reverberate in the client's world. There is a great emotional investment and attachment to the items that are collected,

---

[‡] http://www.digitaljournal.com/article/311930
[§] http://www.npr.org/templates/story/story.php?storyId=104350808

no matter how worthless or trivial they may seem to us. We are therefore faced with a dilemma. How do we help someone to trim down their belongings, when their energy is focused on keeping what they got, as well as adding new things? Your illustration is an excellent case and point. The client finds value in his collected papers, pamphlets and other items, because he sees them as essential toward fulfilling his future aspirations to run a small business. His hoarding behavior may also be important toward the client feeling a sense of control and managing stress. The best way to address his problematic behavior is for the worker to uphold the meaning and importance of hoarding that the client has found, while jointly problem solving where and to what degree he can collect things, with clear demarcations of what is too much. These measurements are normally based on common sense limits brought on by fire risk, needing a clear passageway to the doors, threat of eviction from landlord, or a variety of other health and safety issues. Basic measuring tools like a specific set of shelves or drawers for certain items are agreed upon. Anything beyond these agreed upon limits is removed to another location whether it is given away, thrown away, or put into storage. When this is done in a sensitive manner with client involvement, it is possible, though still difficult, to draw up a cognitive-behavioral plan to manage hoarding.

Regular apartment visits paired with a clear plan on how to cope and re-organize is essential. There is a very straightforward Hoarding Risk Assessment that can be found online, called HOMES. It is a nice way of getting an initial and brief assessment to help conceptualize the hoarding issue with a particular client. Tenancy preservation programs connected with housing courts can also play a vital role in mediating a landlord tenant dispute and getting a counselor with some training in managing hoarding issues to do apartment visits. The housing court can provide a regulated check-in and leverage point for the counselor, the client and the landlord to share progress toward making the apartment safe. Other helpful Hoarding resources and information can be found as follows:

- http://www.tufts.edu/vet/hoarding/pubs/HOMES_SCALE.pdf
- http://www.ocfoundation.org/hoarding/
- https://www.masshousing.com/

The core of our work is about understanding people's narratives and being very responsive to them, which begins with building a trusting relationship and a common language of an agreed-upon set of goals to jointly work on. If we are to serve those with major disabilities, then we need to do the hard work of rolling up our sleeves and providing the outreach and advocacy that is necessary to be effective. In essence, this is what you are doing! You've entered the "client's world" and understand what his needs and challenges are. One major issue among many is his propensity to hoard. Beyond addressing difficulties with hoarding, there are a couple of suggestions to consider. It sounds like he could benefit from a visiting nurse, as well as outreach home care services that help with Activities of Daily Living (ADL) skills, such as medication management, hygiene-bathing and toileting, apartment cleaning, cooking, etc. There are at least two ways besides you or the current case manager to get this kind of help for the gentleman in need.

The first is that Medicaid (State Health Insurance) may fund these services directly via private or private/non-profit nursing and/ or homecare agencies that can bill the client's insurance. In Massachusetts, we use visiting nurse services that also provide homecare services to work on ADL skills. You don't have to be homeless to qualify for this. All you need is the state's version of Medicaid and a primary doctor's authorization, so it can be billed.

The second is via an umbrella state agency that serves people with developmental issues. Each state tends to have specific HHS (Health and Human Services) funds that go toward addressing disabilities, ranging from Major Developmental Disorders to Severe Mental Illnesses. Eligibility for these types of programs can be a challenging process, but most states have a range of case management services to serve people with developmental disabilities and/or severe mental illnesses. Some types of disabilities don't qualify for these services, so you would need to find out what does and see if it is a match for the type of developmental issues the person you are working with has. If he is connected with one of these umbrella state agencies, then they may directly connect him with the type of nursing and homecare services he needs.

Finally, perhaps it is worth advocating with the agency that is providing the case management to see if they can help set up and/or fund the higher intensity outreach services that are needed.

In closing, once things get a bit more settled... perhaps some work can be done to support the client's aspirations to have a small business or to do some sort of related work. Due to his developmental issues, he may qualify for vocational programming. There are state-funded vocation options for individuals that can be found at http://askjan.org/cgiwin/TypeQuery.exe?902.

Even without the help of formal vocational services, there may be creative ways to support the client's career interests and goals. Supporting a person's journey to find meaningful structure in the world regardless of functional level is of utmost importance and should be an integrated part of our attempt to help others.

Michell: Jay, thanks so much! It was a great pleasure doing this interview with you and I hope to stay connected for other case and scenario's discussions. You have taken time out of your busy schedule and we greatly appreciate it. Big Hugs to you!

Jay Levy: Thanks Michell! I'd like to thank you and the *Journal of Humanitarian Affairs* for the opportunity to share my thoughts with your readers.

~

For more information, visit his website: www.JaySLevy.com

Permissions for re-publication granted via Green Heritage News Network: Special Thanks to Ernest Dempsey, Editor of GHN www.GreenHeritageNews.com

References

All Roads Lead Home, (2008). The Pioneer Valley's Plan to End Homelessness. Supported by the Cities of Holyoke, Northampton, Springfield, MA. Funded by One Family, Inc.

Aviles, A. M., & Helfrich, C. A. (2006). Homeless youth: Causes, consequences and the role of occupational therapy. *Occupational Therapy in Health Care*, 20(3-4), 99-114.

Anthony, W., Cohen, M., & Farkas, M. (1990). *Psychiatric rehabilitation*. Boston University: Center For Psychiatric Rehabilitation.

Bender, K., Thompson, S. J., McManus, H., Lantry, J., & Flynn, P. M. (2007, February). Capacity for survival: Exploring strengths of homeless street youth. In *Child and Youth Care Forum* (Vol. 36, No. 1, pp. 25-42). Kluwer Academic Publishers-Plenum Publishers.

Burt, M.R.and Aron, L.Y. (2000). *America's homeless II: Populations and services*. Washington, DC: The Urban Institute.

Burt, M.R., Aron, L.Y., Douglas, T., Valente, J., Lee, E., Iwen, B. (1999, August). Homelessness: Programs and the people they serve. *Findings of a national* survey of homeless assistance: 1996 summary report. Washington, DC: The Urban Institute.

Common Ground Website (2012) Housing First Research: http://www.commonground.org/mission-model/our-results/ & http://www.commonground.org/mission-model/why-common-ground-works/

Culhane, D. P. and Metraux S. (2008, Winter). Rearranging the deck chairs or reallocating the life boats? *Journal of the American Planning Association*, (74)1, 111-121

Dempsey, E., Levy, J.S. & Spolden, M. (2012). Homelessness in America (interview). *The Journal of Humanitarian Affairs* at http://greenheritagenews.com/homeless-outreach-who-qualifies-for-help-as-homeless/

Domestic Violence Resource Center Statistics retrieved from http://www.dvrc-or.org/domestic/violence/resources/C61/

Durso, L.E., & Gates, G.J. (2012). Serving Our Youth: Findings from a National Survey of Service Providers Working with Lesbian, Gay, Bisexual, and Transgender Youth who are Homeless or At Risk of Becoming Homeless. Los Angeles: The Williams Institute with True Colors Fund and The Palette Fund.

Einstein, A. (1981). *The human side: New glimpses from his archives. New Jersey:* Princeton University Press.

Epston, D., and White, M. (1992). *Experience, contradiction, narrative, and* imagination: Selected papers of David Epston and Michael White, 1989-1991. Adelaide, Australia: Dulwich Centre Publications.

Erikson, E.H. (1968). *Identity: youth and crisis.* New York: Norton.

Farrow, J.A., Deisher, R.W., Brown, R., Kulig, J.W. & Kipke, M. (1992). Health and health needs of homeless and runaway youth. *Journal of Adolescent Health,* 13, 717-726.

Frankl, V.E., (1985). *Man's search for meaning.* New York: Washington Square Press.

Freedman, J., & Combs, G. (1996). *Narrative therapy: The social construction of preferred realities.* New York: W. W. Norton Company, Inc.

Gandhi, M.K. (2000). *The words of Gandhi: Second edition.* New York: New Market Press.

Germain, C.B., & Gitterman, A. (1980). *The life model of social work process.* New York: Columbia University Press.

Gladwell, M. (2006). Million Dollar Murray: Why problems like homelessness may be easier to solve than to manage. *The New Yorker,* February 13 & 20, 2006 edition.

Gulcur, L., Stefanie, D., Shinn, M., Tsemberis, S. & Fischer, S. (2003) Housing, hospitalization, and cost outcomes for homeless individuals with psychiatric disabilities participating in continuum of care and Housing First programs. *Journal of Community and Applied Social Psychology,* 12(2), 171–186.

Heidegger, M., (1971). *On the way to language.* trans. Hertz, P. New York: Harper & Row.

Home and Healthy for Good Report (2010). Compiled by Massachusetts Housing & Shelter Alliance Staff. Retrieved

from   website:
http://www.mhsa.net/matriarch/MultiPiecePageText.asp?
PageID=60&PageN ame=HomeHealthyforGoodArchive

*HUD Annual Homeless Report, (2012). 2012 Annual Homeless
Assessment Report to Congress.* Retrieved from website:
https://www.onecpd.info/resources/documents/2012AHA
R_PITestimates.pdf

Hwang, S.W., Lebow, J.J., Bierer, M.F., O'Connell, J., Orav, E.J., and
Brennan, T.A.(1998). Risk factors for deaths in homeless
adults in Boston. *Archives of Internal Medicine,* 158(13):
1454-1460.

James, W. (1907) *Pragmatism: A new name for some old ways of
thinking.* New York: Longmans, Green and Company.

Kegan, R. (1982). *The evolving self: Problem and process in human
development.* Cambridge, MA: Harvard University Press.

Keller, H. (1903). *Optimism: An essay.* TY Crowell.

Kenney, R.R. & Shapiro, L. (2009). *PATH Technical Assistance
Resource Page: Transition Age Youth* (2nd ed). Rockville, MD:
Center for Mental Health Services, Substance Abuse and
Mental Health Services Administration.

Kuhn, R. and Culhane, D. P. (1998) Applying cluster analysis to test of
a typology of homelessness: Results from the analysis of
administrative data. *American Journal of Community
Psychology* 17:1 , 23-43.

Levy, J.S. (1998, Fall). Homeless outreach: A developmental model.
Psychiatric Rehabilitation Journal, 22(2), 123-131.

Levy, J.S. (2000, July-Aug.). Homeless outreach: On the road to
pretreatment alternatives. Families in Society: *The Journal of
Contemporary Human Services,* 81(4), 360-368.

Levy, J.S. (2004). Pathway to a common language: A homeless
outreach perspective. Families in Society: *The Journal of
Contemporary Human Services,* 85(3), 371-378.

Levy, J.S. (2010). *Homeless narratives & pretreatment pathways:
From words to housing.* Ann Arbor, MI: Loving Healing Press.

Levy, J.S. (2011). *Homeless outreach & housing first: Lessons learned.*
Ann Arbor, MI: Loving Healing Press.

Massachusetts Housing and Shelter Alliance (2008). MHSA
Achievements: C-SPECH partnership with Mass Behavioral
Health Plan (MBHP). Retrieved from
http://www.mhsa.net/matriarch/MultiPiecePage.asp_Q_PageID

_E_27_A_PageName_E_accomp

McKinney-Vento Program Eligibility Form (2002) HUD definition of Chronic Homelessness.

McManus, H.H. and Thompson, S.J. (2008). Trauma among unaccompanied homeless youth: The integration of street culture into a model of intervention. *Journal of Aggression, Maltreatment & Trauma,* 16(1), 92-109.

Miller, W.R. & Rollnick, S. (1991). *Motivational interviewing: Preparing people to* change addictive behavior. New York: Guilford.

National Alliance to End Homelessness (2000). *A plan not a dream: How to end homelessness in 10 years.* Retrieved from website: www.endhomelessness.org/pub/tenyear/10yearplan.pdf.

National Alliance to End Homelessness (2006). *Fundamental issues to prevent and end youth homelessness.* Washington, DC: National Alliance to End Homelessness.

National Alliance to End Homelessness (2008). *Incidence and vulnerability of LGBTQ homeless Youth.* Washington, DC: National Alliance to End Homelessness.

National Alliance to End Homelessness (2009). *Homeless youth and sexual exploitation:* Research, findings and practice implications. Washington, DC: National Alliance to End Homelessness.

National Alliance to End Homelessness (2012). Changes in the HUD definition of homeless. www.endhomelessness.org/library/entry/changes-in-the-hud-definition-of-homeless

O'Connell, J.J. *Premature Mortality in Homeless Populations: A Review of the Literature,* 19 pages. Nashville: National Health Care for the Homeless Council, Inc., 2005.

O'Connell, J.J, Swain S. Rough sleepers: A five year prospective study in Boston, 1999-2003. Presentation, Tenth Annual Ending Homelessness Conference, Massachusetts Housing and Shelter Alliance, Waltham, MA 2005.

Pearson, C., Montgomery, A. & Locke, G. (2009) Housing stability among individuals with serious mental illness participating in Housing First programs. *Journal of Community Psychology,* 37(3), 404–417.

Persig, R. M. (1991). *Lila: An inquiry into morals.* New York, New York: Bantam Books.

Piaget, J. (1957). *Construction of reality in the child*. London: Routledge & Kegan Paul.

Pope, L (2009). *Housing for homeless youth*. Washington, DC: National Alliance to End Homelessness.

Prochaska, J.O., & DiClemente, C.C. (1982). Trans theoretical therapy: Toward a more integrative model of change. Psychotherapy: Theory, Research, and *Practice*. 19, 276-288.

Ray, N. (2006). *Lesbian, gay, bisexual and transgender youth: An epidemic of homelessness*. New York: National Gay and Lesbian Task Force Policy Institute and the National Coalition for the Homeless.

Robertson, M.J. & Toro, P.A. (1998). *Homeless youth: Research, intervention, and policy*. Washington, DC: US Department of Health and Human Services.

Rogers, C.R. (1957). The necessary and sufficient conditions for therapeutic personality change. *Journal of Consulting Psychology*, 21, 95-103.

Stefancic, A., & Tsemberis, S. (2007). Housing first for long-term shelter dwellers with psychiatric disabilities in a suburban county: A four-year study of housing access and retention. *The Journal of Primary Prevention*, 28(3-4), 265-279.

SAMHSA & National Homeless Resource Center (1997). *In from the cold: A tool kit for* creating safe havens for people on the streets. Washington, DC: HHS : HUD

Schneir, A., Stefanidis, N., Mounier, C., Balin, D., Carmichael, H. & Battle, T. (2007). *Culture and trauma brief: Trauma among homeless youth*. Los Angeles, CA: National Child Traumatic Stress Network.

Toro, P.A., Dworsky, A. & Fowler, P.J. (2007). Homeless youth in the United States: Recent research findings and interventions. In D. Dennis, G. Locke, & J. Khadduri

(Eds.), *Toward Understanding Homelessness: The 2007 National Symposium on Homelessness Research*. Washington, DC: Office for Assistant Secretary for Planning and Evaluation.

Tsai, J., Mares, A. & Rosenheck, R. (2010) A Multisite Comparison of Supported Housing for Chronically Homeless Adults: "Housing First" Versus "Residential Treatment First". *Psychological Services*, 7(4), 219–232.

Tsemberis, S. (2010) Housing First: Ending homelessness, promoting recovery and reducing cost. In Ellen, I. & O'Flaherty, B. (2010)

(eds) *How to House the Homeless*. New York: Russell Sage Foundation.

Tsemberis, S. & Eisenberg, R. (2000) Pathways to housing: supported housing for street-dwelling homeless individuals with psychiatric disabilities. *Psychiatric Services*, 51(4), 487–493.

Tsemberis, S., Gulcur, L. & Nakae, M. (2004) Housing first, consumer choice, and harm reduction for homeless individuals with a dual diagnosis. *American Journal of Public Health*, 94(4), 651–656.

US Department of Education (2012). Homeless Students Enrolled File Specifications. http://find.ed.gov/search?client=default_frontend&site=default_collection&output=xml_no_dtd&proxystylesheet=default_frontend&q=homeless+youth+definition&sa.x=24&sa.y=14

US Department of Health and Human Services (2008). Runaway and Homeless Youth Act. www.findyouthinfo.gov/youth-topics/runaway-and-homeless-youth/federal-definitions

van Dyke, H. (1909). *The white bees and other poems*. New York: Charles Scribner and Sons.

Walter, J. & Peller, J. (1992). *Becoming solution-focused in brief therapy*. Chicago: Brunner/Mazel.

Wampold, B.E. (2001) *The great psychotherapy Debate: Models, methods, findings*. Mahwah, New Jersey: Lawrence Erlbaum Associates.

Wasserman, J. A. and Clair, J. M. (2010). *At home on the street: People, poverty &a hidden culture of homelessness*. Boulder, Colorado: Lynne Rienner Publishers.

About the Author

Jay S. Levy has spent the last twenty-five years working with individuals who experience homelessness. He is the author of the highly acclaimed book *Homeless Narratives & Pretreatment Pathways: From Words to Housing* and has published a monograph and several journal articles on the subject. His latest publication is entitled *Pretreatment Guide to Homeless Outreach & Housing First: Helping Couples, Youth, and Unaccompanied Adults*. He has helped to develop new Housing First programs such as the Regional Engagement and Assessment for Chronically Homeless Housing First program (REACH). This was adopted by the Western Massachusetts Regional Network as an innovative approach toward reducing chronic homelessness and has also been integrated into the Pioneer Valley's 10-Year Plan to End Chronic Homelessness.

Jay received his MSW degree in clinical social work from Columbia University during 1988. He has achieved formal recognition from the Commonwealth of MA Department of Mental Health for his ongoing efforts to help under-served homeless individuals through his direct service, clinical supervision of staff, and program development. Jay is currently employed by Eliot CHS-Homeless Services as a Regional Manager for the statewide SAMHSA-PATH Homeless Outreach Program and Eliot's Western MA Housing First Program.

Jay lives in Western MA with his wife Louise and his two children, Talia and Sara. He is also an avid stargazer. Further information about homelessness, past and present publications, latest reviews, and interviews are available at his website: www.jayslevy.com

Index

Also from Jay S. Levy

Levy crafts stories of characters who sear the memory: Old Man Ray, the World War II veteran who resents the VA system and regards himself as the de facto night watchman at Port Authority; Ben who claims to be a prophet disowned in his own country, crucified by the government and enslaved by poverty finds a bridge to the mainstream services and a path to housing through the common language of religious metaphors, including redemption and forgiveness; and Andrew who has been 'mentally murdered' is helped to understand his own situation and gain disability benefits through the language of trauma; among others.

"These stories are deftly interwoven with theory and practice as Levy constructs his developmental model of the engagement and pretreatment process. The outreach worker strives to understand the language and the culture of each homeless individual, builds a bridge to the mainstream services, and helps those providers to understand the special circumstances of these vulnerable people. Levy bears witness to the courage of these pilgrims who wander the streets of our cities, and his poignant book is a testament to the healing power of trusting and enduring relationships."
--Jim O'Connell, MD, President and Street Physician
Boston Health Care for the Homeless Program

Homeless Narratives & Pretreatment Pathways: From Words to Housing
Hardcover ISBN 978-1-61599-027-6
Paperback ISBN 978-1-61599-026-9
eBook ISBN 978-1-61599-946-0

From Loving Healing Press

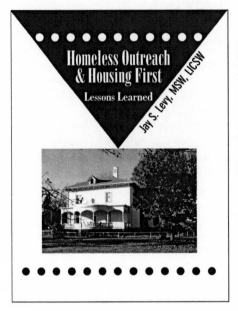

Jay S. Levy brings us a new educational resource entitled *Homeless Outreach & Housing First: Lessons Learned*. This monograph features three written works on homelessness inclusive of an article on moral, fiscal, and quality of life considerations, a new story entitled "Ronald's Narrative: The Original Housing First", and an interview that was originally featured in *Recovering The Self*. These three documents provide a rich and fertile resource for learning, reflecting, and informing needed action that promotes high quality outreach services and housing stabilization for the most vulnerable among us.

The Reader will...

- Learn about the positive measurable impact of a Housing First approach and its moral, fiscal, and quality of life implications.

- Explore the relationship between Homeless Outreach and Housing First, as well as understand the five basic pretreatment principles that can be applied to both.

- Learn how to utilize a Pretreatment Approach with individuals experiencing major mental illness and addiction.

- Understand how to better integrate Housing First and Homeless Outreach initiatives with homelessness policy.

"This is one of the best guides I have read about working with the underserved and homeless. I wonder why all cities don't put it into place? How we approach our homeless can definitely make a difference. Sometimes it's not in the techniques, but in the attitude of the case manager."
--Carol S. Hoyer, PhD, for Reader Views

Homeless Outreach & Housing First: Lessons Learned

Paperback ISBN 978-1-61599-136-5
eBook ISBN 978-1-61599-137-2

From Loving Healing Press

CPSIA information can be obtained at www.ICGtesting.com
Printed in the USA
BVOW04*0316250913

332082BV00004B/104/P